HALAKHIC MAN

HALAKHIC MAN

Rabbi Joseph B. Soloveitchik

Translated from the Hebrew by LAWRENCE KAPLAN

THE JEWISH PUBLICATION SOCIETY

Philadelphia *5743 · 1983*

Library of Congress Cataloging in Publication Data
Soloveitchik, Joseph Dov.
  Halakhic man.

  Translation of: Ish ha-halakhah, galui ve-nistar.
  Includes bibliographical references.
  1. Jewish way of life. 2. Judaism. 3. Jewish law—
Philosophy. I. Title.
BM723.S6613   1983   296.7   83–291

Designed by A D R I A N N E O N D E R D O N K D U D D E N

Cloth, ISBN 0–8276–0222–7
Paper, ISBN 0–8276–0397–5
10 9 8 7 6 5 4 3 2 1

Contents

Translator's Preface

R ABBI Joseph B. Soloveitchik's essay *Ish ha-halakhah—Halakhic Man*—is a unique, almost unclassifiable work. Its pages include a brilliant exposition of Mitnaggedism, of Lithuanian religiosity with its emphasis on Talmudism; a profound excursion into religious psychology and phenomenology; a pioneering attempt at a philosophy of Halakhah; a stringent critique of mysticism and romantic religion in general; as well as anecdotal family history—all held together by the force of the author's highly personal vision.

Perhaps the best description of *Halakhic Man* is that of Eugene Borowitz, who termed it a "Mitnagged phenomenology of awesome proportions." Existentialist motifs are also not lacking. Then again, the work, with its sprinkling of late-nineteenth and early-twentieth-century liberal, apologetic motifs, may, in part, be seen as a halakhic, neo-Kantian cum existential version of Leo Baeck's great essay, "Romantic Religion." Indeed, there is more than a little resemblance between Baeck's images of classical and romantic religion and R.* Soloveitchik's portraits of halakhic man and *homo religiosus*. Nor should the clearly anti-Christian thrust of both essays be overlooked.

---

*In the manner of talmudic and rabbinic designation, "R." denotes "Rabbi."

The wide-ranging nature of *Halakhic Man* calls forth, nay requires, the full deployment of R. Soloveitchik's vast erudition. From a discussion of a biblical or talmudic passage he may smoothly and almost imperceptibly move to an analysis of modern scientific method, then turn to an exposition of Aristotelian or Maimonidean philosophy, buttressed by appropriate modern historical scholarship, follow up with references to modern secular and religious phenomenology and existentialism, and cap the discussion with an acute resolution of a knotty halakhic issue, citing appropriate medieval and modern rabbinic scholarship. Heidegger, Kant, Hermann Cohen, Scheler, Barth, Cassirer, Einstein, Planck, and Niebuhr rub elbows with the Gaon of Vilna, R. Shneur Zalman of Lyady, R. Hayyim Volozhin, R. Isaac of Karlin, R. Joseph Babad, R. Lipele of Mir, R. Isaac Blaser, R. Naphtali Zevi Yehudah Berlin, R. Hayyim Heller, and the members of R. Soloveitchik's own distinguished rabbinic family: his grandfathers, R. Hayyim Soloveitchik and R. Elijah of Pruzhan; his uncles, R. Menahem Krakowski and R. Meir Berlin (Bar-Ilan); and his father, R. Moses Soloveitchik. Above this colorful and varied throng hovers Maimonides, both the Maimonides (or, perhaps better, the Rambam) of the *Mishneh Torah* and the Maimonides of the *Guide of the Perplexed,* together with his "armor-bearers," medieval and modern, *aḥaronim* and practitioners of *Judische Wissenschaft.*

This rich substance finds its appropriate echo in the essay's allusive and complex literary style. R. Soloveitchik, in a brilliant, virtuoso manner, has drawn upon the full resources of the Hebrew language, in all of its layers and transformations, from biblical to modern times. Skillfully interwoven into the texture of the essay are biblical and talmudic phrases, midrashic allusions and halakhic terms, plays on Maimonidean statements, and images from Bialik's poems. Moreover, R. Soloveitchik has varied the tone of his writing in accordance with the variations in substance. Certainly the terse, exceptionally concise and compact, almost elliptic and telegraphic style R. Soloveitchik deems appropriate for a halakhic analysis of the laws of mourning of the high priest differs from the more expansive and dramatic, but still sober and restrained, style he adopts for an analysis of the methodology of modern science or of the personality of cognitive man. And the shift in tone will be more radical when R. Soloveitchik moves from rigorous and abstract analysis, be it halakhic or philosophic, phenomenological or religious, to rapturous poetic outbursts, delicate descriptions of nature, or revealing personal family history. Here we encounter a densely metaphorical, highly charged, and elaborately wrought prose, almost romantic in its luxuriance and passion.

In sum, both in terms of substance and style, *Halakhic Man* is a formidable work, so formidable, indeed, that when first asked to translate the essay, I, not unnaturally, hesitated. And, indeed, had not R. Soloveitchik, generously and graciously, consented to review the translation, my initial hesitation might have proved decisive. I am deeply grateful to him both for affording me so much of his own valuable time and for the many stylistic infelicities and substantive errors from which he saved me. Naturally in all those instances where I have either misrepresented or failed to convey R. Soloveitchik's meaning, where I have muffled a nuance or missed an allusion, where, above all, I have not succeeded in capturing his unique literary voice, the fault remains my own. I do trust, however, that at least some measure of both R. Soloveitchik's voice and his vision has made its way across the inadequate medium of translation.

Ish ha-halakhah, in its original language, has been issued in three different editions. It first appeared in 1944 in the journal *Talpiot* (vol. 1, nos. 3–4, pp. 651–735). Subsequently, the essay was published in the volumes *Be-sod ha-yaḥid ve-ha-yaḥad*, ed. Pinhas Peli (Jerusalem: Orot, 1976) and *Ish ha-halakhah—galuyi ve-nistar* (Jerusalem: World Zionist Organization, 1979). Although I consulted all three versions, which except for minor modifications are identical, the present translation is based on the edition of the World Zionist Organization.

My rendering aims to be a faithful reflection of the original Hebrew text. However, in the course of the effort I undertook some minor, but, I trust, useful adjustments. It became evident that R. Soloveitchik, in some instances, cited texts from memory, with occasional inexactitudes. In such cases I corrected both the citations and the references, translating the original text. Second, though R. Soloveitchik provides the sources for many of his citations, not all such references are given. Thus, I have offered the sources for all biblical citations which the author omitted entirely, as well as for all the talmudic, midrashic, philosophic, and other citations whose sources were left unnoted. These additional sources, in the case of biblical quotations, appear in parentheses; the other sources in brackets. I have also followed standard referencing procedure and have given full bibliographical information for all sources, where these seemed insufficiently noted. These additions, too, are indicated by brackets, as are elaborations, where I thought this might be helpful, of terms, concepts, and allusions. Finally, in order to make the notes more comprehensible to the nonspecialist I paraphrastically expanded the author's highly compressed halakhic argumentation, oftentimes, indeed, interpolating explanatory material. This, too, is indicated by brackets.

Translations of biblical texts, it should be remarked, follow the *Holy Scriptures* issued by The Jewish Publication Society of America (1917); in some few instances, however, the JPS rendition has not been observed, where the context of the passage required a different translation, or to reflect a particular interpretation. For translations of talmudic and midrashic passages I consulted the Soncino versions of the Talmud and Midrash Rabbah, and for translations of passages from Maimonides's *Mishneh Torah*, the various translations of the *Yale Judaica Series*. My translations, however, generally differ from these renditions, sometimes slightly, sometimes radically. All quotations from Maimonides's *Guide of the Perplexed* are from the translation by Shlomo Pines (Chicago University Press, 1963).

It now remains only to thank a few people: Moshe Lichtenstein for his hospitality and thoughtfulness; Mrs. Louis Granitch for her efficient typing of the manuscript; my colleague, Professor Eugene Orenstein, for his help in translating the excerpt from Peretz in note 114; Professor Isadore Twersky, son-in-law of R. Soloveitchik, for overseeing the entire project, setting down the general guidelines, and providing me with always helpful advice; Maier Deshell for his editorial skill and, even more important, for his patience, tact, and friendship; my wife, Feige, for giving me the crucial initial encouragement that enabled me to overcome my original, very real, hesitations; and above all, my own teacher, the halakhic man, par excellence, of our generation, R. Joseph B. Soloveitchik. I have already thanked him for the time and effort and, indeed, profound intellectual energy and creativity he expended in reviewing my translation. I wish only to add that I am proud both to have been his student and to have been given the opportunity of introducing *Halakhic Man,* his first great essay and a modern intellectual, spiritual, and religious classic, to an English-reading audience.

LAWRENCE KAPLAN

At that moment the image of his father came to him and appeared before him in the window.

—SOTAH 36b

PART ONE

HALAKHIC MAN

His World View and His Life

H ALAKHIC man[1] reflects two opposing selves; two disparate images are embodied within his soul and spirit. On the one hand he is as far removed from *homo religiosus* as east is from west and is identical, in many respects, to prosaic, cognitive man; on the other hand he is a man of God, possessor of an ontological approach that is devoted to God and of a world view saturated with the radiance of the Divine Presence. For this reason it is difficult to analyze halakhic man's religious consciousness by applying the terms and traits that descriptive psychology and modern philosophy of religion have used to characterize the religious personality.

The image that halakhic man presents is singular, even strange. He is of a type that is unfamiliar to students of religion. But if, in the light of modern philosophy, *homo religiosus* in general has come to be regarded as an antithetical being, fraught with contradictions, who wrestles with his consciousness and struggles with the tribulations of the dualism of affirmation and negation, approbation and denigration, how much more so is this true of halakhic man? In some respects he is a *homo religiosus*, in other respects a cognitive man. But taken as a whole he is uniquely different from both of them.

Halakhic man is an anti-nomic type for a dual reason: (1) he bears within the deep recesses of his personality the soul of *homo religiosus*, that soul which, as was stated above, suffers from the pangs of self-contradiction and self-negation; (2) at the same time halakhic man's personality also embraces the soul of cognitive man, and this soul contradicts all of the desires and strivings of the religious soul. However, these opposing forces which struggle together in the religious consciousness of halakhic man are not of a destructive or disjunctive nature. Halakhic man is not some illegitimate, unstable hybrid. On the contrary, out of the contradictions and antinomies there emerges a radiant, holy personality whose soul has been purified in the furnace of struggle and opposition and redeemed in the fires of the torments of spiritual disharmony to a degree unmatched by the universal *homo religiosus*. The deep split of the soul prior to its being united may, at times, raise a man to a rank of perfection, which for sheer brilliance and beauty is unequaled by any level attained by the simple, whole personality who has never been tried by the pangs of spiritual discord. "In accordance with the suffering is the reward" [Avot 5:23] and in accordance with the split the union! This spiritual fusion that characterizes halakhic man is distinguished by its consummate splendor, for did not the split touch the very depths, the innermost core, of his being? There is much truth to the fundamental contention set forth both by the dialectical philosophies of Heraclitus[2] and Hegel with regard to the ongoing course of existence in general and the views of Kierkegaard, Karl Barth,[3] and Rudolf Otto with regard to the religious consciousness and its embodiment in the experience of *homo religiosus*—in particular, namely, that there is a creative power embedded within antithesis;[4] conflict enriches existence, the negation is constructive, and contradiction[5] deepens and expands the ultimate destiny of both man and the world.

Our aim in this essay is to penetrate deep into the structure of halakhic man's consciousness and to determine the precise nature of this "strange, singular" being who reveals himself to the world from within his narrow, constricted "four cubits" [Berakhot 8a], his hands soiled by the gritty realia of practical Halakhah [see Berakhot 4a]. However, in order to fulfill the task we have set before us in this monograph, we must undertake a comparative study of the fundamental and distinctive features of the ontological outlooks of *homo religiosus* and cognitive man. For only by gaining an insight into the differences and distinctions existing between these two outlooks will we be able to comprehend the nature of halakhic man, the master of talmudic dialectics.

II

HOW radically different is the approach of *homo religiosus* to God's world from that of cognitive man! When cognitive man observes and scrutinizes the great and exalted cosmos, it is with the intent of understanding and comprehending its features; cognitive man's desire is to uncover the secret of the world and to unravel the problems of existence. When theoretical and scientific man peers into the cosmos, he is filled with one exceedingly powerful yearning, which is to search for clarity and understanding, for solutions and resolutions.[6] Cognitive man aims to solve the problems of cognition vis-à-vis reality and longs to disperse the cloud of mystery which hangs darkly over the order of phenomena and events.

Cognitive man does not tolerate any obscurity, any oblique allusions and undeciphered secrets in existence. He desires to establish fixed principles, to create laws and judgments, to negate the unforeseen and the incomprehensible, to understand the wondrous and the sudden in existence. Cognitive man establishes a cosmic order characterized by necessity and lawfulness. Any phenomenon which cannot be subjected to the rule of law and principle is relegated to the realm of the nonbeing and nothingness (μὴ ὄν) of the Platonists or, at best, to the hylic matter (δύναμις or ὕλη) posited by Aristotle.

The common denominator of both the Platonic and Aristotelian views is that the random and the particular are not deemed worthy of being granted the status of the real and existent and remain in the realm of chaos and the void. Only that which is fixed, clear, and ordered, only that which is engraved with the imprint of lawful reality merits the appellation and title of true or effective being (ὄντως ὄν or ἐνέργεια) in which the idea (ἐιδος) participates. The attitude of disdain and contempt to that which is not fixed, not lawful, and not ordered—which was so prevalent in the teachings of the Greek philosophers and which found its most acute expression in the philosophies of Plato and Aristotle—is the eternal Greek legacy to all cognitive and scientific men. The alpha and omega of existence is its lawfulness. To be sure, the concept of lawfulness assumes different forms, depending upon the philosophical mood of the age and the perspective of inquiry. Throughout the Middle Ages, in accordance with the Aristotelian approach, the concept of lawfulness was identified with the immanent teleological process of the idea (ἐιδος) or the forms (μορφή). With the arrival of modern classical physics, the concept of lawfulness was identified with the mechanical causality formulated by Galileo and Newton. More recently, the modern metaphysical school, which concerns itself with the absolute, has espoused a (neo-Aristotelian) concept of the lawfulness of the essences. However, no matter how diverse these various concepts of causality are, they all reveal the basic tendency of cognitive man: the search for the ordered and fixed in existence. He is profoundly engaged in rendering an accounting of the world and charts out for himself a structured plan of reality enclosed in borders of order and law, whose ultimate status cannot be denied. Cognition, for him, consists in discovering the secret, solving the riddle, hidden, buried deep in reality, precisely through the cognition of the scientific order and pattern of the world. In a word, the act of cognitive man is one of revelation and disclosure.

The *homo religiosus* acts differently.[7] When he confronts God's world, when he gazes at the myriads of events and phenomena occurring in the cosmos, he does not desire to transform the secrets embedded in creation into simple equations that a mere tyro is capable of grasping. On the contrary, *homo religiosus* is intrigued by the mystery of existence—the *mysterium tremendum*—and wants to emphasize that mystery. He gazes at that which is obscure without the intent of explaining it and inquires into that which is concealed without the intent of receiving the reward of clear understanding.

The dynamic relationship that exists between the subject-knower and the object-known expresses itself, for *homo religiosus,* not in the desire and ability of the subject to comprehend the object but, on the contrary, in accepting the fascinating, eternal mystery that envelops the object.

This is not to say that *homo religiosus* prefers the chaos and the void to the structured cosmos or that he would choose to undo the act of creation and introduce confusion into reality. Heaven forbid! *Homo religiosus,* like cognitive man, seeks the lawful and the ordered, the fixed and the necessary. But for the former, unlike the latter, the revelation of the law and the comprehension of the order and interconnectedness of existence only intensifies and deepens the question and the problem. For while cognitive man discharges his obligation by establishing the reign of a causal structure of lawfulness in nature, *homo religiosus* is not satisfied with the perfection of the world under the dominion of the law. For to him the concept of lawfulness is in itself the deepest of mysteries.

Cognition, according to the world view of the man of God, consists in the discovery of the wondrous and miraculous quality of the very laws of nature themselves. The mystery of the world is to be encountered precisely in the understanding of the functional relationship in effect between the phenomena of this world. Every clarification of a phenomenon brings in its wake new enigmas. *Homo religiosus* sees the entire ordered world, the entire creation which is delimited and bound by the law as a cryptic text whose content cannot be deciphered, as a conundrum that the most resourceful of men cannot solve.

The riddle of riddles is the very nature of the law itself. In a word, the cognitive act of *homo religiosus* is one of concealment and hiding.

III

IN truth these two attitudes parallel the twofold nature of existence itself. The ontological dualism is a reflection of an ontic dualism.

Reality possesses two faces. On the one hand, she presents us with a bright, happy, smiling face; she greets us with a cheerful countenance and reveals to us something of her essence. She grants us permission to gaze upon her and peer at her image. She shows us a bit of her lawful structure and the order of her actions. In such moments of grace and compassion the object submits itself to the subject, the thing to the person, reality—to man who forms an inextricable part of it, existence—to intellect and knowledge. Here there blossoms forth the wondrous relationship between subject and object, cognizer and cognized. The process of cognition, the problem of problems and enigma of enigmas of man, reveals itself in all its splendor and majesty. And it is this act of grace, this act of disclosure, which nature, at times, performs for our benefit, that is at the root of all human culture.

On the other hand, however, reality is possessed of an extreme modesty; at times she conceals herself in her innermost chamber and disappears from the view of the scholar and investigator. Everything bespeaks secrets and enigmas, everything—wonders and miracles. And reality is characterized by a strange feature. For, at the very moment when she treats us generously and reveals to us a bit of her form, she covers much much more. The problem increases as the cognition progresses. The neo-Kantian philosophers have given striking expression to this ancient idea when they said that the function that holds between the solution and the problem is analogous to the function that holds between the radius and circumference of a circle and its area. As the radius and circumference increase arithmetically,[8] the area increases geometrically.[9] Existence plays a mischievous game with us, as though to tease and provoke us. In the midst of knowledge there yet once again arises the mystery; in the midst of contemplation the riddle gains new strength. As was stated above, all scholarly scientific attainments derive from the "candid, open, and obliging" aspect of reality. From its modest and retiring aspect, however, stream forth all the oppositions and contradictions in cognition, all the antinomies in that image of the cosmos which is revealed to us, all the unsolvable problems, and all of the irrationality and strangeness which at times appears to us in that picture of reality that hovers before our eyes.

As emphasized above, the ontic dualism is transformed into an ontological dualism. The duality in the attitudes of cognitive man and *homo religiosus* is rooted in existence itself. Cognitive man concerns himself with a simple and "candid" reality. He does not seek to closet himself with the hidden in existence but rather focuses his attention on its revealed aspect. This is not the case with *homo religiosus*. He clings to a reality which, as it were, has removed itself from the cognizing subject and has barred the intellect from all access to it. He is totally devoted and given over to a cosmos that is filled with divine secrets and eternal mysteries. The very nature of the law itself, the very phenomenon of cognition is an open book for cognitive man and a closed one for *homo religiosus*.[10]

When God appears to Job out of the whirlwind, He asks him: "Where wast thou when I laid the foundations of the earth? Declare, if thou hast the understanding. Who determined the measures thereof, if thou knowest? Or who stretched the line upon it? Whereupon were the foundations thereof fastened? Or who laid the cornerstone thereof? . . . Have the gates of death been revealed unto thee, etc.? Hast thou entered the treasuries of the snow, etc.? Dost thou know the time when the wild goats of the rock bring forth, etc.? Doth the hawk soar by thy wisdom, etc.?" (Job 38, 39). The consciousness of *homo religiosus* is overflowing with questions that will never be resolved. He scans reality and is overcome with wonder, fixes his attention on the world and is astonished. Moreover, the astonishment that overwhelms *homo religiosus* does not serve simply as a prod to stimulate metaphysical curiosity, is not just a device to excite the cognitive imagination—i.e., is not just a means to an end, as Aristotle thought, but is the ultimate goal and crowning glory of the process of cognition of *homo religiosus*.

And Job, who had raged against heaven because he had sought to render an accounting of the world and erred, accepts upon himself the divine judgment. "Who is it that hideth counsel without knowledge? Therefore have I uttered that which I understood not, things too wonderful for me, which I knew not" (Job 42:3). He sinned with his proud and overly bold venture to grasp and comprehend the secret of the cosmos; he confesses and returns to God with the discovery of the mystery in the created world and of his inability to understand that mystery. "Wherefore I abhor my words, and repent, seeing I am dust and ashes" (Job 42:6). The ultimate goal of religious man is the question, Dost thou know? The path which leads him to his aim is the complete cognition of being.[11] A strange polarity of disclosure and hiding, revealing and concealing, breaks forth and seizes hold of the consciousness of the man of God. He discloses in order to hide, reveals in order to conceal.

Therefore this stance is devoid of the slightest trace of that agnostic doctrine which denies objectivity to knowledge and effaces the truth and validity of the cognitive act. The viewpoint that has been described here neither brings the religious individual to rebel against the kingdom of knowledge and cognition nor does it lead him to adopt that exaggerated and distorted position of Tertullian, *"credo quia absurdum est"* (I believe because it is absurd),[12] a position born out of the bitter despair and terrible disillusionment of a man who, with his intellect, knocks upon the gates of the universe that stand shut and locked before him. On the contrary, *homo religiosus* is eager to cognize natural phenomena and understand them, but knowledge itself for him is the greatest and most difficult riddle of all. Knowledge and wonder, cognition and mystery, understanding and secrecy, the law and the unknown, these constitute a unified phenomenon which reveals itself to us in a twofold fashion, all in accordance with one's perspective and point of view. However, knowledge does not forfeit its objective status and intrinsic significance as a result of the *teiku*, the unresolvable problem that peers out of its windows. On the contrary, the riddle adorns and embellishes cognition, bestowing upon it the splendor of eternity.

In this respect the teaching of our great master, Maimonides (of blessed memory), is typical. On the one hand, Maimonides ruled that the knowledge of God is the first among the 613 commandments. "The foundation of foundations and the pillar of all sciences is to know that there is a prime being . . . and this knowledge is a positive commandment."[13] On the other hand, he maintained the doctrine of negative attributes, which denies all possibility of knowing God. On the one hand, Maimonides designated the knowledge of the Creator as the guiding criteria for man, as his ultimate end. On the other hand, Maimonides held the view that knowledge of God is not in the realm of human cognition. Are there two greater opposites then these? Nevertheless! Maimonides himself struggled with this antinomy and devoted two chapters of the *Guide of the Perplexed* (I:59–60) to it. The substance of his answer is that negative cognition does not forfeit its status as cognition. However, we know[14] that the entire phenomenon of negative cognition is only possible against a backdrop of affirmative cognition. For we negate with respect to the Creator all of the attributes that we have affirmed with respect to created beings.

Therefore, in order to arrive at the negation, we must engage in an act of affirmation. The act of negation is reconstructed out of the very substance of affirmation. And what constitutes affirmative cognition if not the cognition of the cosmos—the attributes of action? Moses prayed that these attributes be communicated to him, and his petition was granted. Indeed, we are all commanded to occupy ourselves with the understanding in depth of these attributes, for they bring us to the love and fear of God, as Maimonides explains in the *Laws of the Foundations of the Torah* (II, 2). First we cognize in positive categories God's great and exalted world, and afterward we negate the attributes of created beings from the Creator. This solution accords well with the ontological approach of the man of God: cognition for the sake of grasping the eternal riddle, revealing for the sake of concealing, comprehending for the sake of laying bare the incomprehensible in all its glorious mystery and terror. The negative theology constitutes the great ideal of *homo religiosus;* it is the "telos" of his noetic process (which will never and can never be entirely realized) and the "end point" of his knowledge—the cognition of the riddle without end (negative cognition) through affirmative cognition. It is for the purpose of the unending realization of this idea that *homo religiosus* has been commanded to engage profoundly in rendering an account of the world, to occupy himself with the "natural science" and the "divine science," and this cognition is entirely affirmative and not negative. To be sure, negation is always distantly visible as the goal and final aim of knowledge; however, the process of cognition itself from its "beginning" until its "end" takes on shape in a whirl of colors against an affirmative backdrop. Negation is only the actualization of the cognitive process and the realization of the act of affirmative cognition in its fullness. The old familiar proverb of negative theology—"the goal of knowledge is to know not"—refers, as is clear from the proverb itself, only to the goal and the aim but not to the process of cognition. The knowledge of God which leads to love and fear, concerning which we were commanded in the *Laws of the Foundations of the Torah,* is the cognition of the attributes of action—the cosmos—and this cognition is entirely affirmative.[15]

IV

THIS characteristic attitude of *homo religiosus* toward existence directly entails the following conclusion: *homo religiosus* does not acknowledge any ontic monism. Reality for him is not uniform and monochromatic but rather pluralistic and multilayered. Ontic pluralism is the very foundation of the world view of *homo religiosus.* When he approaches the world in order to cognize and evaluate it, he attempts to find in this concrete and physical world the traces of higher worlds, all of which are wholly good and eternal. He seeks to discover the source of the plenitude in being and of the fullness of the cosmos in supernal ontic realms that are pristine and pure. This transcendent approach to reality constitutes a primary feature of the profile of the man of God. *Homo religiosus* is dissatisfied, unhappy with this world. He searches for an existence that is above empirical reality. This world is a pale image of another world.

Cognitive man, on the other hand, is not concerned at all with a reality that extends outside the realm of lawfulness, and he has no relationship with any mode of being that is beyond empirical reality and scientific understanding—for the law is his goal, and lawfulness is always and only to be found within a context of concreteness. In his *Critique of Pure Reason,* Kant established the bounds of space and time as the limits of comprehension. Cognitive man pays no attention to and is wholly uninterested in a world that is above the rule of empirical reality. The object with which he is concerned is completely hemmed in by the total physical and psychical reality.

But *homo religiosus* passes beyond the realm of concreteness and reality set within the frame of scientific experience and enters into a higher realm.

Indeed, the echo of the longings of *homo religiosus* for a supernal existence succeeds, from time to time, in making itself heard in the world of knowledge and science. The world of ideas of Plato as the paradigm of true being, and the realm of the phenomena as the shadows of being; the ascent, in the ontological doctrine of Aristotle, from the first hylic matter (which cannot be conceived) to the first pure form; the noetic cosmos in the system of Philo; the concept of emanation and the multiplicity of worlds which proceed from one another according to the Neoplatonic school; the infinite substance consisting of infinite attributes on the one hand, and the two attributes of extension and thought which are known to us on the other in Spinoza's philosophy; the phenomena and the absolute (noumena) in Kantianism; the revival of the dualism of essence and existence, which was so prevalent in Arabic philosophy and Christian Scholasticism, in the phenomenological approach of Husserl and Scheler; the modern metaphysics which attempts to penetrate to absolute being; the entire doctrine of epistemological idealism which subjects existence to thought and consciousness in all of the various forms in which it unfolded from Berkeley to Hermann Cohen; the concept of absolute values which won for itself such an important place in modern ethical and epistemological theories; etc., etc.—all constitute traces of religious thought, which yearns for its Creator and rebels against the concrete reality that so entirely surrounds it. A soul overwhelmed by religious longings may, at certain times, stray amid the paths of secular knowledge.

This religious quest, however, does not confine itself solely to theoretical stances and abstract views but breaks out of the theoretical realm into the realm of praxis and utility. The search for transcendence is transformed into an ethical principle; it turns into a pillar of fire that lights the path before the religious individual.

The ladder of ethical perfection, like the biblical ladder of Jacob, is set fast upon the earth, upon the ground of concrete reality, and the top of it reaches unto the very heavens. The ethical and religious ideal of *homo religiosus* is the extrication of his existence from the bonds of this world, from the iron chains of empirical reality, its laws and judgments, and its elevation up to the level of being of a higher man, in a world that is wholly good and wholly eternal. The aim of religion is to liberate those who are bound in fetters and irons, those who dwell in darkness and gloom—"the king held captive in tresses" (Songs 7:6)—and crown them all with the royal crown of a supernal, transcendental existence, emanating from holy, eternal realms.

This motif winds its way through the whole experiential fabric of *homo religiosus*. Of course, this tendency takes on various, at times contradictory, forms. Sometimes the craving for transcendence clothes itself in an ascetic garb, in an act of negation of life and of this world, in a denial of the worthwhile nature of existence. The longing of *homo religiosus* for a supernal world that extends beyond the bounds of concrete reality has been embodied in many doctrines of asceticism, renunciation, and self-affliction. At such moments *homo religiosus* is of the opinion that sufferings and torments, fasting and seclusion are the means which convey eternal felicity to man and bring him under the wings of the supernal. The individual who forgoes worldly pleasures and renounces temporal life will merit, according to this view, eternal life and a lofty, exalted existence.

At other times this motif may assume an extreme form of affirmation of the world and approval of reality. However, even according to this stance, concrete, empirical reality serves only as a springboard from which man may make his plunge into the supernal, and it is the supernal realm alone that serves as the object of the religious individual's deepest longing, the goal of his ultimate quest. Naturally, between the two extremes of asceticism on the one hand and affirmation of the world on the other, there are a number of intermediate positions that graft together elements from both stances and create hybrid religious and moral systems.

From a philosophical perspective the difference between the approach of self-affliction and that of affirmation of reality is purely an ethical-practical one, rooted in the act of evaluating earthly life as a means for the realization of the goal. From an ontological standpoint, and also from the perspective of the ethical ideal, the two are similar. Both proceed from the same theoretical perspective, both relate to a multilayered existence, both acknowledge an ontic and ontological pluralism, and both see in the striving for a higher form of existence the symbol of ethical perfection. The entire opposition between a doctrine of asceticism and a doctrine that affirms and rejoices in life's pleasures centers on the practical-utilitarian stance to be adopted and pertains to the means for bringing about the realization of the ethical ideal. The former states that the negation of life raises man to an elevated level and to the very heights of true existence while the latter disagrees and is of the opinion that only through accepting the yoke of the dominion of empirical reality may we hope to merit a more exalted existence.

These attitudes toward reality are prevalent both in pantheistic and theistic systems. Each system naturally impresses its own stamp upon the ethical conclusions that flow from the approach of *homo religiosus* to transcendence, and the various conclusions are by no means similar.

The common denominator of all of them is that *homo religiosus* longs for a refined and purified existence. The riddle in existence and the eternal problem that hovers over the face of being leads him beyond the bounds of concrete reality.

V

HALAKHIC man differs in his world view from the universal *homo religiosus*. He resembles in various ways cognitive man, yet, he differs in many respects from him as well.

Halakhic man's approach to reality is, at the outset, devoid of any element of transcendence. Indeed, his entire attitude to the world stands out by virtue of its originality and uniqueness. All of the frames of reference constructed by the philosophers and psychologists of religion for explaining the varieties of religious experience cannot accommodate halakhic man as far as his reaction to empirical reality is concerned. Halakhic man studies reality not because he is motivated by plain curiosity the way theoretical man is; nor is he driven to explore the world by any fear of being or anxiety of nonbeing. Nor, for that matter, does halakhic man orient himself to the world in terms of a nebulous feeling of absolute dependence, or yearnings for the redemption of man, or visions of a great, revealed ethical ideal. Halakhic man orients himself to reality through a priori images of the world which he bears in the deep recesses of his personality. We may, if we so desire, call this a cognitive-normative approach, but it is not to be identified with the cognitive and ethical orientation of which the philosophers, the cognitive men par excellence, speak.[16]

We know that cognitive man has a dual relationship to reality: (1) an empirical, a posteriori approach; (2) an a priori approach. And it need not be emphasized that the entire dispute between rationalists and empiricists centers around this problem. In truth this disagreement symbolizes two different directions in man's relationship to reality. When cognitive man scrutinizes God's world and seeks, through critical probing, to determine its nature (I am not concerned here with the nature of the cause that precipitates cognition), he arrives at two differing decisions: (1) To plunge into the very midst of reality and to contemplate its appearance in order to understand its essence and structure. Cognitive man, in this instance, approaches the world without preconceived programs, without any elaborate preparations. He gropes in the darkness, is astonished and amazed by the plethora of phenomena and by the "chaos and void" which prevail in the realm of reality, until he stumbles across a repetition of events in a certain order, which he had dimly sensed to begin with, as a result of which he can construct rules and establish laws that can serve as a beacon illuminating the road on which he travels through the cosmos.[17] (2) In order to overcome the mystery in existence, he constructs an ideal, ordered, and fixed world, one that is perfectly clear and lucid; he fashions an a priori, ideal creation with which he is greatly pleased. This creation does not cause him any anxiety. It does not attempt to elude him; it can not conceal itself from him. He knows it full well and delights in the knowledge. Whenever he wishes to orient himself to reality and to superimpose his a priori ideal system upon the realm of concrete empirical existence, he comes with his teaching in hand—his a priori teaching. He has no wish to passively cognize reality as it is in itself. Rather, first he creates the ideal a priori image, the ideal structure, and then compares it with the real world. His approach to reality consists solely in establishing the correspondence in effect between his ideal, a priori creation and concrete reality. More, even when the theoretician with his a priori system gets involved in the technological, utilitarian aspects of science, there, too, his sole aim is to reveal the parallelism that prevails between the ideal series and the concrete series. And having achieved this aim he has fulfilled his task. For he is concerned not with the concrete, qualitative phenomena themselves but only with the relationship that prevails between them and his a priori, ideal constructs.

This latter approach is that of mathematics and the mathematical, natural sciences, the crowning achievement of civilization. It is both a priori and ideal—i.e., to know means to construct an ideal, lawful, unified system whose necessity flows from its very nature, a system that does not require, as far as its validity and truth are concerned, precise parallelism with the correlative realm of concrete, qualitative phenomena. On the contrary, all that we have is an approximate accord. The concrete empirical triangle is not exactly identical with the ideal triangle of geometry, and the same holds true for all other mathematical constructs. There exists an ideal world and a concrete one, and between the two only an approximate parallelism prevails. In truth, not only from a theoretical, ideal perspective does mathematics pay no attention to concrete correlatives, but even from a utilitarian standpoint the mathematical approach has no desire to apprehend the concrete world per se but seeks only to establish a relationship of parallelism and analogy.[18]

VI

WHEN halakhic man approaches reality, he comes with his Torah, given to him from Sinai, in hand. He orients himself to the world by means of fixed statutes and firm principles. An entire corpus of precepts and laws guides him along the path leading to existence. Halakhic man, well furnished with rules, judgments, and fundamental principles, draws near the world with an a priori relation. His approach begins with an ideal creation and concludes with a real one. To whom may he be compared? To a mathematician who fashions an ideal world and then uses it for the purpose of establishing a realationship between it and the real world, as was explained above. The essence of the Halakhah, which was received from God, consists in creating an ideal world and cognizing the relationship between that ideal world and our concrete environment in all its visible manifestations and underlying structures. There is no phenomenon, entity, or object in this concrete world which the a priori Halakhah does not approach with its ideal standard. When halakhic man comes across a spring bubbling quietly, he already possesses a fixed, a priori relationship with this real phenomenon: the complex of laws regarding the halakhic construct of a spring. The spring is fit for the immersion of a *zav* (a man with a discharge); it may serve as *mei ḥatat* (waters of expiation); it purifies with flowing water; it does not require a fixed quantity of forty se'ahs; etc. [See Maimonides, *Laws of Immersion Pools,* 9:8.] When halakhic man approaches a real spring, he gazes at it and carefully examines its nature. He possesses, a priori, ideal principles and precepts which establish the character of the spring as a halakhic construct, and he uses the statutes for the purpose of determining normative law: does the real spring correspond to the requirements of the ideal Halakhah or not?

Halakhic man is not overly curious, and he is not particularly concerned with cognizing the spring as it is in itself. Rather, he desires to coordinate the a priori concept with the a posteriori phenomenon.

When halakhic man looks to the western horizon and sees the fading rays of the setting sun or to the eastern horizon and sees the first light of dawn and the glowing rays of the rising sun, he knows that this sunset or sunrise imposes upon him anew obligations and commandments. Dawn and sunrise obligate him to fulfill those commandments that are performed during the day: the recitation of the morning *Shema, tzitzit, tefillin,* the morning prayer, *etrog, shofar, Hallel,* and the like. They make the time fit for the carrying out of certain halakhic practices: Temple service, acceptance of testimony, conversion, *halitzah,* etc., etc. Sunset imposes upon him those obligations and commandments that are performed during the night: the recitation of the evening *Shema, matzah,* the counting of the *omer,*[19] etc. The sunset on Sabbath and holiday eves sanctifies the day: the profane and the holy are dependent upon a natural cosmic phenomenon—the sun sinking below the horizon. It is not anything transcendent that creates holiness but rather the visible reality—the regular cycle of the natural order. Halakhic man examines the sunrise and sunset, the dawn and the appearance of the stars; he gazes into the horizon—Is the upper horizon pale and the same as the lower?[20]—and looks at the sun's shadows—Has afternoon already arrived?[21] When he goes out on a clear, moonlit night (until the deficiency of the moon is replenished) he makes a blessing upon it. He knows that it is the moon that determines the times of the months and thus of all the Jewish seasons and festivals, and this determination must rely upon astronomical calculations.

When halakhic man chances upon mighty mountains, he utilizes the measurements which determine a private domain (*reshut ha-yaḥid*): a sloping mound that attains a height of ten handbreaths within a distance of four cubits. When he sees trees, plants, and animals, he classifies them according to their species and genera. Many laws are dependent upon the classification of the species. When a fruit is growing, halakhic man measures the fruit with the standards of growth and ripening that he possesses: budding stage, early stage of ripening, formation of fruits or leaves, and reaching one-third of complete ripeness.[22] He gazes at colors and determines their quality: distinguishes between green and yellow, blue and white, etc., etc., "between blood and blood, between affection and affection" (Deut. 17:8) [i.e. between the various colors of vaginal blood and skin affections; see Rashi ad loc.]. He investigates the matter of the nurturing of trees and plants: the relative importance of the branches vis-à-vis the roots. He approaches existential space with an a priori yardstick, with fixed laws and principles, precepts that were revealed to Moses on Mount Sinai: the imaginary bridging of a spatial gap less than three handbreaths; the imaginary vertical extension, upward or downward, of a partition; the imaginary vertical extension of the edge of a roof downward to the ground; the bent wall; the measurements of four square cubits, ten handbreaths, etc., etc. He perceives space by means of these laws just like the mathematician who gazes at existential space by means of the ideal geometric space.

Halakhic man explores every nook and cranny of physical-biological existence. He determines the character of all of the animal functions of man—eating, sex, and all the bodily necessities—by means of halakhic principles and standards: the bulk of an olive (ke-zayit), the bulk of a date (ke-kotevet), the time required to eat a half-loaf meal (kedai akhilat peras), the time required to drink a quarter log (revi'it), eating in a normal or nonnormal manner, the beginning of intercourse, the conclusion of intercourse, normal intercourse and unnatural intercourse, etc., etc. Halakhah concerns itself with the normal as well as abnormal functioning of the organism, with the total biological functioning of the organism: the laws of menstruation, the man or woman suffering from a discharge, the mode of determining the onset of menstruation, virginal blood, pregnancy, the various stages in the birth process, the various physical signs that make animals or birds fit or unfit for consumption, etc., etc.

There is no real phenomenon to which halakhic man does not possess a fixed relationship from the outset and a clear, definitive, a priori orientation. He is interested in sociological creations: the state, society, and the relationship of individuals within a communal context. The Halakhah encompasses laws of business, torts, neighbors, plaintiff and defendant, creditor and debtor, partners, agents, workers, artisans, bailees, etc. Family life—marriage, divorce, halitzah, sotah, conjugal refusal (mi'un), the respective rights, obligations, and duties of a husband and a wife—is clarified and elucidated by it. War, the high court, courts and the penalties they impose—all are just a few of the multitude of halakhic subjects. The halakhist is involved with psychological problems—for example, sanity and insanity, the possibility or impossibility of a happy marriage, *miggo* [i.e., the principle that a party's plea gains credibility when a more advantageous plea is available], and assumptions as to the intention behind a specific act (*umdana*), the presumption that a particular individual is a liar or a sinner, the discretion of the judges,[23] etc., etc. "The measure thereof is longer than the earth and broader than the sea" (Job 11:9).

Halakhah has a fixed a priori relationship to the whole of reality in all of its fine and detailed particulars. Halakhic man orients himself to the entire cosmos and tries to understand it by utilizing an ideal world which he bears in his halakhic consciousness. All halakhic concepts are a priori, and it is through them that halakhic man looks at the world. As we said above, his world view is similar to that of the mathematician: a priori and ideal. Both the mathematician and the halakhist gaze at the concrete world from an a priori, ideal standpoint and use a priori categories and concepts which determine from the outset their relationship to the qualitative phenomena they encounter. Both examine empirical reality from the vantage point of an ideal reality. There is one question which they raise: Does this real phenomenon correspond to their ideal construction?[24]

And when many halakhic concepts do not correspond with the phenomena of the real world, halakhic man is not at all distressed. His deepest desire is not the realization of the Halakhah but rather the ideal construction which was given to him from Sinai, and this ideal construction exists forever. "There never was an idolatrous city and never will be. For what purpose, then, was its law written? Expound it and receive a reward! There never was a leprous house and never will be. For what purpose, then, was its law written? Expound it and receive a reward! There never was a rebellious son and never will be. For what purpose, then, was his law written? Expound it and receive a reward!"[25] Halakhic man is not at all grieved by the fact that many ideal constructions have never been and will never be actualized. What difference does it make whether the idolatrous city, the leprous house, and the rebellious son existed or didn't exist in the past, will exist or won't exist in the future? The foundation of foundations and the pillar of halakhic thought is not the practical ruling but the determination of the theoretical Halakhah. Therefore, many of the greatest halakhic men avoided and still avoid serving in rabbinical posts. They rather join themselves to the group of those who are reluctant to render practical decisions. And if necessity—which is not to be decried—compels them to disregard their preference and to render practical decisions, this is only a small, insignificant responsibility which does not stand at the center of their concerns.

The theoretical Halakhah, not the practical decision, the ideal creation, not the empirical one, represent the longing of halakhic man.[26] Halakhic man engages in theoretical discussion and debate concerning the subjects of sacrifices and purity and plumbs the depths of those concepts, laws, and distinctions with the same seriousness that he investigates and searches out the laws of *agunah*, plaintiff and defendant, and forbidden foods. The yeshivah of Volozhin introduced the study of the entire Talmud from beginning to end—from Berakhot to Niddah—in place of the previous practice of skipping over those tractates which do not deal with laws that are practiced nowadays. R. Hayyim Soloveitchik, aside from his regular lecture at the yeshivah of Volozhin, would also deliver a parallel lecture on the tractates Zevaḥim [animal offerings] and Menaḥot [meal offerings]. When he would deliver a lecture on the tractate Eruvin [partitions vis-à-vis the Sabbath laws], he also dealt with the Mishnaic treatise Ohalot [tents]—[which is concerned with partitions vis-à-vis] the laws of corpse defilement. When he studied the tractate Berakhot [blessings], he also dealt with agricultural laws, even though those laws, inasmuch as they are dependent upon the land of Israel, are not practiced outside the land. A significant part of his halakhic novella is devoted to laws of sacrifice and purity and defilement. Rabbi Naphtali Zevi Yehudah Berlin acted in a similar fashion, as did many Torah giants both before and after them. This stance has been a fundamental characteristic of halakhists from time immemorial.[27]

Rashi, the Tosafists, and the other Ashkenazic and Sephardic scholars devoted a large part of their prodigous powers also to matters that are not practiced nowadays. Maimonides in his great code of law, *Yad Ha-Ḥazakah,* codified all of the laws of the Torah from the first mishnah in Berakhot to the last mishnah in Uktzin. And with the same precision and the same rigorous standards that he used in determining the law in the case of a man who lent money to his fellow and said, "Do not pay me save in the presence of so and so,"[28] or in the case of a man who deposited with his fellow an unmeasured mass of produce and the bailee commingled it with his own produce without measuring it,[29] or in the case of a bailee who was negligent with regard to landed property,[30] etc., etc., laws that are bound up with the everyday life of our people, he also treated the order of the service of the high priest on the Day of Atonement, the laws of the Passover sacrifice, the disqualification of certain sacrifices brought about by being left overnight, Nazariteship, the red heifer, the defilement of the corpse and the leper, etc., etc. Will the mathematician worry that the ideal, irrational number does not correspond to the real number? Both the halakhist and the mathematician live in an ideal realm and enjoy the radiance of their own creations. "When a person understands and grasps any halakhah in the Mishnah or Gemara fully and clearly ... and now this halakhah is the wisdom and will of the Holy One, blessed be He, for it is His will that in case Reuben pleads thus, for example, and Simon thus, the decision should be thus; and even if such a case involving these particular pleas never came before a court and will never come, nevertheless, since it has been the will and the wisdom of the Holy One, blessed be He, that in case a person pleads thus and another person pleads thus, then the decision shall be thus; therefore, when a person knows and grasps with his intellect this decision in accordance with the law as set forth in the Mishnah, Gemara, or Codes, he thereby comprehends, grasps, and encompasses with his intellect the will and wisdom of the Holy One, blessed be He, whom no thought can grasp, etc."[31]

The concept of the Day of Atonement or the night of Passover, for example, is an ideal concept, and halakhic man sees the Day of Atonement in the resplendent image of the glory of the sacrificial service of the day or the night of Passover in all its majesty, at the time when the Temple was still standing. Both the Day of Atonement and the Passover festival nowadays, when we have no high priest, nor sacrifices, nor altar and the whole Temple service cannot take place, are devoid of all that holiness and glory with which they were endowed at the time of the Temple. Both are only a pale image of the ideal constructions that were given on Mount Sinai.[32]

When Maimonides describes the order of events on the fifteenth night of Nisan, he "forgets" temporarily that he is living approximately one thousand years after the destruction of the Temple and paints the image of the service of this holy festival night in a wealth of colors that dazzle the eye, that reflect the Passover service as it was celebrated thousands of years ago in ancient Jerusalem and as it once again will be celebrated in the era of the Messiah. Thus writes Maimonides in *The Laws of Hametz and Matzah,* 8:1: "The order in which the aforementioned commandments should be fulfilled on the night of the fifteenth [of Nisan] is as follows: First a cup is mixed for each person and he recites the blessing 'who has created the fruit of the vine' and he recites over it the sanctification of the day and drinks." This formulation is known to us from *Orah Hayyim, Hayyei Adam,* the prayerbook of R. Jacob Emden, the prayerbook *Derekh Hayyim* of R. Jacob Lissa, the abridged *Shulhan Arukh,* and similar works, and its very ring recalls to mind the ditty *Kadesh u-rehatz,* so familiar to all schoolchildren. It would seem that *The Laws of Ḥametz and Matzah,* chapter 8, and an illustrated Haggadah which one can buy for a few pennies differ only in style and phraseology. However, as we continue to read we suddenly come across a "peculiar" *seder:* "And afterward he recites the blessing . . . and a table, ready laid, is brought in bearing a bitter herb and another vegetable, unleavened bread, *ḥaroset,* and the body of the paschal lamb and meat from the festival offering of the day of the fourteenth." Maimonides did not intend to set down the order of the performance of the commandments on the night of the fifteenth for the benefit of his generation, but rather for the pilgrims who went up to Jerusalem, who roasted their paschal lambs and ate them with thanksgiving and praise. Similarly, when Maimonides continued his description, "And a second cup of wine is mixed and at that point the son asks, 'Why is this night different from all other nights? . . . For on all other nights we eat meat roasted, stewed, or boiled, but on this night it is all roasted,'" he had in mind not the innocent child of his own day who would recline at his father's table in Cairo or Cordova, where there was neither a paschal offering nor a festival offering, but rather the son who reclined at his father's table in ancient Jerusalem on the holy festival night, when the air would resound with the tones of the *Hallel* recited over the eating of the paschal lamb. And Maimonides's text continues in this fashion later on: "The table is then replaced in front of him and he says: 'This paschal offering that we eat is on account . . .' and afterward he recites the blessing 'Blessed art Thou, O Lord our God, King of the universe, who has sanctified us with His commandments and commanded us concerning the eating of the festival offering.' And he eats first from the festival offering, then he recites the blessing 'Blessed . . . concerning the eating of the paschal offering' and he eats some of the body of the paschal offering, etc. Finally he eats [some more] of the meat of the paschal offering even if only an olive's bulk and does not taste anything more." The *seder* with which Maimonides is

On whole relig neatly to rec apt to ideal &
we lack the temption.

dealing is an ideal conception of Passover night. Our great master pays no attention to the cruel and bitter present. The picture of a restored Jerusalem, the Temple in all its splendor, the priests at their service, and free Israelites performing the commandments of the night hovers before his eyes. However, from time to time he bestirs himself from his ideal dream and romantic vision and finds himself confronted with an exile filled with nightmares and terrors, with physical oppression and spiritual degeneration, and he states: "In the present time he does not say, 'tonight it is all roasted,' for we no longer have any paschal offering, etc. And in the present time he says, 'The Passover offering which our fathers used to eat when the Temple was standing,' etc., and in the present time one adds 'So, O Lord our God . . . bring us to other festivals . . . happy in the building of the city and joyous in Thy service. And there may we eat of the sacrifices and the paschal offerings,' etc. In the present time when there is no offering, after he recites the blessing 'He who brings forth bread from the earth,' etc., and in the present time he eats an olive's bulk of *matzah* and does not taste anything more after that." In other words, the present time is only a historical anomaly in the ongoing process of the actualization of the ideal Halakhah in the real world, and there is no need to elaborate about a period which is but a temporary aberration that has seized hold of our historical existence. The Halakhah remains in full force, and we hope for and eagerly await the day of Israel's redemption when the ideal world will triumph over the profane reality.

And when halakhic man stands up and prays, "May it be Thy will . . . that Thou wilt replenish the deficiency of the moon and it will no longer be diminished" [in the prayer following the blessing over the new moon], he refers to the replenishing of the deficiency of the real cosmos which does not correspond to the ideal image of reality. Halakhic man's yearnings for the national redemption, for the coming of the Messiah, and for the building of the eternal Temple draw upon his hidden longings for the full and complete realization of the ideal world in the very nub of concrete reality, for that era when the Halakhah will shine in all its majesty and beauty, in the midst of our empirical world. Then all of life will benefit from the image of this exalted and resplendent divinely willed construction.[33]

Halakhic man's ideal is to subject reality to the yoke of the Halakhah. However, as long as this desire cannot be implemented, halakhic man does not despair, nor does he reflect at all concerning the clash of the real and the ideal, the opposition which exists between the theoretical Halakhah and the actual deed, between law and life. He goes his own way and does not kick against his lot and fate.

Such is also the way of the mathematician! When Riemann and Lobachevski discovered the possibility of a non-Euclidean space, they did not pay any attention to the existential space in which we all live and which we encounter with all our senses, which is Euclidean from beginning to end. They were concerned with an ideal mathematical construction, and in that ideal world they discerned certain features of a geometric space different from ours. Afterward, physicists such as Einstein and his circle appeared, and they utilized the concept of a non-Euclidean space in order to explain certain physical phenomena. The ideal-geometric space then found its actualization in the real world. (However, according to modern epistemological doctrine, and as many leading mathematical physicists such as Hertz, Einstein, Planck, and Eddington have admitted, even the physicist does not simply photograph reality, but rather creates a world of constructs that only parallels a concrete, empirical correlative.)

VII

[margin note: transcendence.]

HALAKHIC man's relationship to transcendence differs from that of the universal *homo religiosus*. Halakhic man does not long for a transcendent world, for "supernal" levels of a pure, pristine existence, for was not the ideal world—halakhic man's deepest desire, his darling child—created only for the purpose of being actualized in our real world? It is this world which constitutes the stage for the Halakhah, the setting for halakhic man's life. It is here that the Halakhah can be implemented to a greater or lesser degree. It is here that it can pass from potentiality into actuality. It is here, in this world, that halakhic man acquires eternal life! "Better is one hour of Torah and *mitzvot* in this world than the whole life of the world to come," stated the tanna in Avot [4:17], and this declaration is the watchword of the halakhist. Not only will the universal *homo religiosus* not understand this statement, but he will have only contempt for it, as if, heaven forbid, it intended to deny the pure and exalted life after death. The story is told about the Gaon of Vilna, how just before his death he clutched the *tzitzit* of his garment, wept, and exclaimed: "How beautiful is this world—for one penny a person can acquire eternal life." And when a Polish woman of noble birth proved stubborn and demanded, as the purchase price for the fresh, green, moist myrtles that grew in her garden, the reward that was reserved for the Gaon for the performance of the commandment, he gladly and wholeheartedly fulfilled her request and "transferred" to her the reward for the commandment of taking the four species. On that Sukkot, so the folk legend relates, he was exceedingly joyful and told his students: "All my life I grieved, when would I have the opportunity of fulfilling a commandment without receiving a reward, in order that I might thereby fulfill the injunction of Antigonos of Socho: 'Be like the servants

[margin note: Better! hr of Torah in this life then all worlds to come.]

who minister to their master without the intent of receiving a reward' [Avot 1:31]; and now that I have this opportunity, should I not fulfill this commandment with gladness and joy?"

Judaism has a negative attitude toward death: a corpse defiles; a grave defiles; a person who has been defiled by a corpse is defiled for seven days and is forbidden to eat any sacred offerings or enter the Temple; a Nazarite who has been defiled by a corpse cancels his previous count and must carry out the shaving of his head for defilement and bring an offering; the priests of God are forbidden to defile themselves with the dead. He whose holiness is of a higher order than the holiness of his fellow is subject to a more severe prohibition against defilement. An ordinary priest may defile himself for his seven relatives, the high priest (and similarly the Nazarite) may not defile himself even for them.[34]

Many religions view the phenomenon of death as a positive spectacle, inasmuch as it highlights and sensitizes the religious consciousness and "sensibility." They, therefore, sanctify death and the grave because it is here that we find ourselves at the threshold of transcendence, at the portal of the world to come. Death is seen as a window filled with light, open to an exalted, supernal realm. Judaism, however, proclaims that coming into contact with the dead precipitates defilement. Judaism abhors death, organic decay, and dissolution. It bids one to choose life and sanctify it. Authentic Judaism as reflected in halakhic thought sees in death a terrifying contradiction to the whole of religious life. Death negates the entire magnificent experience of halakhic man. "'I am free among the dead' (Ps. 88:6)—when a person dies, he is freed from the commandments" [Shabbat 30a]. The customary Jewish practice to act like the people of Lorraine who removed the *tzitzit* from the shrouds of the dead constitutes authoritative teaching.[35] To repeat, Halakhah is devoid of any positive orientation to death and burial; on the contrary, it views these phenomena from a negative perspective. "One whose dead [relative] lies before him is exempt from the recital of the *Shema* and from prayer and from *tefillin* and from all precepts laid down in the Torah" [Berakhot 3:1]. The Tosafists, in order to explain this law, cite the statement of R. Bun in the Palestinian Talmud [Berakhot 3:1 (5d)]: "It is written 'that thou mayest remember the day when thou camest forth out of the land of Egypt all the days of thy life' (Deut. 16:3). [The commitment accepted in Egypt is only applicable] to man who is preoccupied with life and not to one who has encountered death." (Rashi, ad loc., and Maimonides in his *Commentary on the Mishnah,* ad loc., are, however, of the opinion that this law stems from the principle that he who is occupied with one commandment is exempt from all other commandments.)

Death is the symbol of the most intense defilement; therefore he who is holy is unto his Lord must keep far away from such defilement. Thus the Scriptures declare with regard to the high priest: "He shall not defile himself for his father, or for his mother, for his brother, or for his sister, when they die; because his consecretion unto God is upon his head" (Num. 6:7).

The Halakhah is not at all concerned with a transcendent world. The world to come is a tranquil, quiet world that is wholly good, wholly everlasting, and wholly eternal, wherein a man will receive the reward for the commandments which he performed in this world. However, the receiving of a reward is not a religious act; therefore, halakhic man prefers the real world to a transcendent existence because here, in this world, man is given the opportunity to create, act, accomplish, while there, in the world to come, he is powerless to change anything at all. "Whosoever has prepared on the eve of Sabbath will eat on the Sabbath" [Avodah Zarah 3a]. The sages taught, qua law revealed to Moses from Mount Sinai, that an animal set apart for a sin offering (*ḥat'at*) whose owner died must be left to die. If the animal was set apart as a guilt offering (*asham*) and the owner dies, the animal is left to graze until it develops a blemish and becomes unfit for sacrifice; then it is sold and its money is used for a burnt offering (olah). Atonement, according to the Halakhah, is only operative within the realm of the concrete life of flesh and blood, of body and soul; it does not penetrate into the domain of transcendent existence.[36]

The task of the religious individual is bound up with the performance of commandments, and this performance is confined to this world, to physical, concrete reality, to clamorous, tumultuous life, pulsating with exuberance and strength. Therefore, holiness need keep itself far away from death. The priest, the Nazarite, the Temple court, holy offerings are all removed, as if by an iron wall, from the realm of death.

Holiness means the holiness of earthly, here-and-now life. "Rabbi Joshua b. Levi said: When Moses ascended on high, the ministering angels spoke before the Holy One, blessed be He, 'Sovereign of the universe! What business has one born of woman among us?' He answered them, 'He has come to receive the Torah.' They said to Him, 'That secret treasure . . . Thou desirest to give to flesh and blood!' . . . The Holy One, blessed be He, said to Moses, 'Return them an answer.' . . . He [then] spoke before Him, 'Sovereign of the universe! The Torah which Thou givest me, what is written therein? *I am the Lord Thy God, who brought thee out of the land of Egypt* (Exod. 20:2).' Said he to them [the angels], 'Did you go down to Egypt? Were you enslaved to Pharaoh?, etc. Again what is written therein? *Remember the Sabbath day, to keep it holy* (Exod. 20:8). Do you then perform work that you need to rest?, etc. Again, what is written therein? *Honor thy father and thy mother* (Exod. 20:12). Do you have any fathers and mothers? Again what is written therein? *Thou shalt not murder. Thou shalt not commit adultery. Thou shalt not steal* (Exod. 20:13). Is there jealousy among you; is the Evil Tempter among you?' Straight away they conceded to Him," etc., etc. [Shabbat 88b–89a]. God does not wish to hand over His Torah to the ministering angels, the denizens of a transcendent world. Rather, he handed over His Torah to Moses, who brought it down to the earth and caused it to dwell among human beings, "who reside in darkness and deep gloom" (Ps. 107:10). The earth and bodily life are the very ground of the halakhic reality. Only against the concrete, empirical backdrop of this world can the Torah be implemented; angels, who neither eat nor drink, who neither quarrel with one another nor are envious of one another, are not worthy and fit for the receiving of the Torah.

"The saving of a life overrides the commandments of the entire Torah; and he shall live by them and not die by them. Desecrate one Sabbath on his account so that he may keep many Sabbaths" [Yoma 85b]. This law is the watchword of Judaism. "An authority who allows himself to be consulted [when a life is in danger] is reprehensible, and he who consults him [rather than speedily acting to save the life in danger] is a murderer" [Tur, *Oraḥ Ḥayyim* 328]. Maimonides, that master of conciseness, deviated from his regular manner and treated this issue with great elaborateness: "When such things have to be done, they should not be left to heathens, minors, slaves, or women. . . . They should rather be done by adult and scholarly Israelites. Furthermore, it is forbidden to delay such violation of the Sabbath for the sake of a person who is dangerously ill. For Scripture says: 'which if a man do, he shall live by them' (Lev. 18:5), that is to say, he shall not die by them. Hence you learn that the ordinances of the Torah were meant to bring upon the world not vengeance, but mercy, lovingkindness, and peace. It is of heretics who assert that this is nevertheless a violation of the Sabbath and therefore prohibited that Scripture says, 'Wherefore I gave them also statutes that were not good, and ordinances whereby they should not live' (Ezek. 20:25)."[37] The teachings of the Torah do not oppose the laws of life and reality, for were they to clash with this world and were they to negate the value of concrete, physiological-biological existence, then they would contain not mercy, lovingkindness, and peace but vengeance and wrath. Even if there is only a doubtful possibility that a person's life is in danger, one renders a lenient decision; and as long as one is able to discover some possible danger to life, one may use that doubt to render a lenient decision. My grandfather, R. Hayyim of Brisk, disagreed with the legal view that on the Day of Atonement one feeds a sick person who is in danger [of dying] small amounts of food at a time, each amount less than the forbidden measure of food for that day. Rather he instructed those who were taking care of a sick individual to serve him a regular meal, just as they would on other days. When my father was about to travel to Rasseyn, a town close to Kovno, to take up a rabbinical post, R. Hayyim took him aside and said, "I command you to follow my view regarding a sick person in danger on the Day of Atonement for it is an absolute halakhic truth." This law that *pikuah nefesh*, saving a life, overrides all the commandments and its far-reaching effects are indicative of the high value which the halakhic viewpoint attributes to one's earthly life—indeed they serve to confirm and nurture that value. Temporal life becomes transformed into eternal life; it becomes sanctified and elevated with eternal holiness.

We have stated that Judaism, as reflected in the Halakhah, has a negative attitude toward death. A person is obligated to rend his garment and mourn for his relative. The Halakhah has established certain units of time with regard to mourning: the first day (on which mourning, according to many *rishonim* [early medieval authorities], is a biblical commandment), seven days, thirty days, twelve months. The *onen*, a mourner on the day of death, is forbidden to eat any sacred offerings; moreover the mourner does not have any sacrifices offered up on his behalf during the entire seven-day mourning period.[38] The high priest is forbidden to let his hair grow and rend his garment for his dead relative,[39] for preoccupation with the memory of the dead desecrates the holiness of the Temple and that of the high priesthood. Indeed many *rishonim* exempted the high priest from all rites of mourning.[40] Holiness is rooted and embedded in joy. "And ye shall rejoice before the Lord your God seven days" (Lev. 23:40), "and thou shalt rejoice in all the good" (Deut. 26:11); "And thou shalt be altogether joyful" (Deut. 16:15). Joy is the symbol of the real life in which the Halakhah is actualized. *Avelut,* mourning, and *aninut,* grief, however, are interwoven and bound up with that arch-opponent of holiness—death. Death and holiness constitute two contradictory verses, as it were, and the third harmonizing verse has yet to make its appearance. The Gaon of Vilna, R. Joseph Dov Soloveitchik, his son, R. Hayyim, his grandson, R. Moses, R. Elijah Pruzna [Feinstein] never visited cemeteries and never prostrated themselves upon the graves of their ancestors. The memory of death would have distracted them from their intensive efforts to study the Torah.

It is only against this background that we can comprehend a peculiar feature in the character of many great Jewish scholars and halakhic giants: the fear of death. Halakhic man is afraid of death; the dread of dissolution oftentimes seizes hold of him. My uncle, R. Meir Berlin [Bar-Ilan], related the following incident to me. Once he and R. Hayyim of Brisk happened to be staying in the same hotel in Libau on the shore of the Baltic. One fine, clear morning he arose at sunrise and went out on the balcony there to find R. Hayyim sitting—his head between his hands, his glance fixed upon the rays of the rising sun, entirely absorbed in the aesthetic experience of such a glorious cosmic spectacle and, at the same time, entirely bent beneath the oppressive weight of a soul-shattering melancholy and a black despair.

R. Berlin took hold of R. Hayyim's shoulder and shook it: "Why are you so troubled and disturbed, my master and teacher? Is something in particular responsible for your distress?"

"Yes," replied R. Hayyim, "I am reflecting upon the end of every man—death."

Halakhic man enjoyed the splendor of sunrise in the east and the swelling sea in the west, but this very experience, which contained in miniature the beauty of the cosmos as a whole and the joy of sheer existence, precipitated in him despair and deep depression. The beauty and splendor of the world on the one hand, and the fate of man, who can enjoy this mysterious magnificence for only a brief, fleeting moment, on the other hand, touched the chords of his sensitive heart, which sensed the entire tragedy concealed with this phenomenon: a great and resplendent world and man, "few of days, and full of trouble" (Job 14:1). The fear of death is transformed here into a quiet anguish, a silent pain, and a tender and delicate sadness that are adorned with the precious embellishment of a profound and lofty aesthetic experience. However, the individual who undergoes such an exalted experience is not the type who longs for transcendence, yearning to break out of the realm of the concrete, for why should such a one be disheartened and grieved on account of the beauty of this world, which is but a pale reflection of a hidden, supernal existence. The halakhic man who gazed at the first rays of the sun and reflected upon the beauty of the world and the nothingness of man in an ecstatic mood of joy intermixed with tragedy is a this-worldly man, an individual given over to concrete reality, who communicates with his Creator, not beyond the bounds of finitude, not in a holy, transcendent realm enwrapped in mystery, but rather in the very midst of the world and the fullness thereof.

"I said: I shall not see the Lord, even the Lord in the land of the living, etc. For the nether-world cannot praise Thee: death cannot celebrate Thee; they that go down into the pit cannot hope for Thy truth. The living, the living, he shall praise Thee, as I do this day; the Father to the children shall make known Thy truth" (Isa. 38:11–19), sang King Hezekiah when he recovered from his illness. "I shall not die, but live, and declare the works of the Lord" (Ps. 118:17), pleaded David, king of Israel, before his Creator. And the echo of these hymns still resounds through the world of Halakhah.[41]

The ideal of halakhic man is the redemption of the world not via a higher world but via the world itself, via the adaptation of empirical reality to the ideal patterns of Halakhah. If a Jew lives in accordance with the Halakhah (and a life in accordance with the Halakhah means, first, the comprehension of the Halakhah per se and, second, comparing the ideal Halakhah and the real world—the act of realization of the Halakhah), then he shall find redemption. A lowly world is elevated through the Halakhah to the level of a divine world.

If a Jew cognizes, for example, the Sabbath laws and the precepts concerning the sanctity of the day in all their particulars, if he comprehends, via a profound study and understanding that penetrates to the very depths, the basic principles of Torah law that take on form and color within the tractate Shabbat, then he will perceive the sunset of a Sabbath eve not only as a natural cosmic phenomenon but as an unsurpassably awe-inspiring, sacred, and exalted vision— an eternal sanctity that is reflected in the setting of the sun. I remember how once, on the Day of Atonement, I went outside into the synagogue courtyard with my father [R. Moses Solo-veitchik], just before the *Ne'ilah* service. It had been a fresh, clear day, one of the fine, almost delicate days of summer's end, filled with sunshine and light. Evening was fast approaching, and an exquisite autumn sun was sinking in the west, beyond the trees of the cemetery, into a sea of purple and gold. R. Moses, a halakhic man par excellence, turned to me and said: "This sunset differs from ordinary sunsets for with it forgiveness is bestowed upon us for our sins" (the end of the day atones).[42] The Day of Atonement and the forgiveness of sins merged and blended here with the splendor and beauty of the world and with the hidden lawfulness of the order of creation and the whole was transformed into one living, holy, cosmic phenomenon.

When the righteous sit in the world to come, where there is neither eating nor drinking, with their crowns on their heads, and enjoy the radiance of the divine presence [cf. Berakhot 17a; Maimonides, *Laws of Repentance* 8:2], they occupy themselves with the study of the Torah, which treats of bodily life in our lowly world. "Now they were disputing in the heavenly academy thus: If the bright spot [of the leper] preceded the white hair, he is defiled; if the reverse, he is clean. If [the order is] in doubt, the Holy One, blessed be He, ruled he is clean; while the entire heavenly academy ruled he is defiled."[43] "When Moses ascended on high, he found the Holy One, blessed be He, studying the pericope of [the red] cow and saying: My son Eliezer says: A heifer [whose neck is to be broken must not be more than] a year old, and a [red] cow [neither more nor less than] two years old."[44] The Creator of worlds, revealed and unrevealed, the heavenly hosts, the souls of the righteous all grapple with halakhic problems that are bound up with the empirical world—the red cow, the heifer whose neck is to be broken, leprosy, and similar issues. They do not concern themselves with transcendence, with questions that are above space and time, but with the problems of earthly life in all its details and particulars. And when the sages stated, "The day consists of twelve hours; during the first three hours the Holy One, blessed be He, sits and occupies Himself with the Torah, etc.,"[45] they referred to the Torah, which was given to us—the Torah, which deals with civil law, forbidden foods, forbidden sexual relations, marriage and divorce, ḥametz and matzah, shofar, lulav, sukkah, and all other similar commandments.

The universal homo religiosus proclaims: The lower yearns for the higher. But halakhic man, with his unique mode of understanding, declares: The higher longs and pines for the lower.

VIII

HOWEVER, at precisely this point, there appears the central antinomy that disturbs the consciousness of halakhic man. On the one hand, as we explained above, his image resembles that of cognitive man, who occupies himself with intellectual constructions—experiencing all the while the joy of discovery and the thrill of creation—and then coordinating his ideal intelligibles with the real world, as does the mathematician. And yet, on the other hand, halakhic man is not a secular, cognitive type, unconcerned with transcendence and totally under the sway of temporal life. God's Torah has implanted in halakhic man's consciousness both the idea of everlasting life and the desire for eternity. As the benediction preceding the reciting of the Torah states: "And everlasting life has He planted in our midst." Halakhic man is also a *homo religiosus* in all his loftiness and splendor. His soul, too, thirsts for the living God, and these streams of yearning surge and flow to the sea of transcendence to "God who conceals Himself in His dazzling hiddenness" [the first line of a kabbalistic piyyut recited at the conclusion of the third Sabbath meal]. One verse states that halakhic man holds fast, with all his being, to the concrete reality of our empirical world, while another verse states that halakhic man reaches out to God and abides under the shadow of the Almighty. How can these two contradictory verses coexist?

The third harmonizing verse states: The only difference between *homo religiosus* and halakhic man is a change of courses—they travel in opposite directions. *Homo religiosus* starts out in this world and ends up in supernal realms; halakhic man starts out in supernal realms and ends up in this world. *Homo religiosus*, dissatisfied, disappointed, and unhappy, craves to rise up from the vale of tears, from concrete reality, and aspires to climb to the mountain of the Lord. He attempts to extricate himself from the narrow straits of empirical existence and emerge into the wide spaces of a pure and pristine transcendental existence. Halakhic man, on the contrary, longs to bring transcendence down into this valley of the shadow of death—i.e., into our world—and transform it into a land of the living. Basically, *homo religiosus* is a romantic who chafes against concrete reality and tries to flee to distant worlds that will restore his spirits with their purity and pristine clarity.[46] Halakhic man, however, takes up his position in this world and does not move from it. He wishes to purify this world, not to escape from it. "Flight goeth before a fall. [Sotah 8:6]" Halakhic man is characterized by a powerful stiff-neckedness and stubbornness. He fights against life's evil and struggles relentlessly with the wicked kingdom and with all the hosts of iniquity in the cosmos. His goal is not flight to another world that is wholly good, but rather bringing down that eternal world into the midst of our world. *Homo religiosus,* his glance fixed upon the higher realms, forgets all too frequently the lower realms and becomes ensnared in the sins of ethical inconsistency and hypocrisy. See what many religions have done to this world on account of their yearning to break through the bounds of concrete reality and escape to the sphere of eternity. They have been so intoxicated by their dreams of an exalted supernal existence that they have failed to hear the cries of "them that dwell in houses of clay" (Job 4:19), the sighs of orphans, the groans of the destitute. Had they not desired to unite with infinity and to merge with transcendence, then they might have been able to do something to aid the widow and orphan, to save the oppressed from the hand of the oppressor. There is nothing so physically and spiritually destructive as diverting one's attention from this world. And, by contrast, how courageous is halakhic man who does not flee from this world, who does not seek to escape to some pure, supernal realm. Halakhic man craves to bring down the divine presence and holiness into the midst of space and time, into the midst of finite, earthly existence.

Halakhic man differs both from *homo religiosus,* who rebels against the rule of reality and seeks refuge in a supernal world, and from cognitive man, who does not encounter any transcendence at all. Halakhic man apprehends transcendence. However, instead of rising up to it, he tries to bring it down to him. Rather than raising the lower realms to the higher world, halakhic man brings down the higher realms to the lower world.

Halakhic man knows that there is no royal road leading to the transcendent realm. Man's whole being is stamped with the indelible imprint of corporeality, concreteness, and sensation. And whither shall he go from their presence, and whither shall he flee from them? Yea, if he ascends to a heavenly existence, there will they be; yea, if he takes the wings of the abstract and the supernal, there would their hand lead him. Halakhic man does not believe that one who is held captive in the prison house of bodily existence can free himself from all vestiges of material existence, can snap the fetters of the body and the *yetzer* and ride in his majesty through the skies.

And more. Halakhic man's religious viewpoint is highly exoteric. His face is turned toward the people. The Torah, whether in terms of study or practice, is the possession of the entire Jewish community. Everyone, from the judges and leaders of the people to the hewers of wood and drawers of water, is obliged to live in accordance with the Torah. "Ye are standing this day, all of you before the Lord your God: your leaders, your tribes, your elders, and your officers . . . from the hewer of thy wood unto the drawer of thy water" (Deut. 29:9–10). The ideal of eternal life is not the private domain of a small spiritual elite or some particularly gifted individuals, but is the public domain of all Israel. "With three crowns was Israel crowned—with the crown of the Torah, with the crown of the priesthood, and with the crown of royalty. Aaron acquired the crown of priesthood. . . . David acquired the crown of royalty. The crown of the Torah, however, is ready and available for all Israel, for it is written: 'Moses commanded us a law, an inheritance of the congregation of Jacob' (Deut. 33:4). Whoever desires it may come and take it."[47] However, spiritual aspirations toward transcendence and fixing one's glance upon a higher world result in the religious world view becoming a religious esotericism which the halakhic understanding of the world refutes from the outset. The generation has not yet arisen that is fit to serve

God through the negation of concrete existence and through casting off of the yoke of the senses and the body. Therefore, any religious ideology that soars upon the wings of the seraphim and the angels on high and abhors mortal man, flesh and blood, will, perforce, in the end (1) prove unfaithful to itself and be guilty of perpetrating a religious lie, as was stated above; (2) constrict itself to a narrow, dark corner, relinquish the public domain, and give rise to a concept of religious esotericism. A religiosity that centers upon the heavenly kingdom and not upon the earthly kingdom—that can be made to reflect the heavenly kingdom—gives rise to ecclesiastical tyranny, religious aristocracies, and charismatic personalities. And there is nothing that the Halakhah loathes and despises as much as the idea of cultic mediation or the choosing of individuals, on the basis of supernatural considerations, to be intercessors for the community.

The thrust of Halakhah is democratic from beginning to end. The Halakhah declares that any religion that confines itself to some remote corner of society, to an elite sect or faction, will give rise to destructive consequences that far outweigh any putative gains. A religious ideology that fixes boundaries and sets up dividing lines between people borders on heresy. If a religion declares that God is close to Reuben (on account of his lineage, profession, or priestly role) and remote from Simeon, it is gravely culpable. No person, according to the Halakhah, needs the aid of others in order to approach God. A person needs no advocates or special pleaders. Every individual is assured by the Halakhah that whenever he will knock on the gates of heaven, they will be opened before him. And just as the Halakhah rejects the notion of human intercessors, so, too, it rejects the notion of transcendental intercessors such as angels and seraphim. One of the thirteen principles of faith, formulated by Maimonides, is "that to Him alone it is fitting to pray, and it is not fitting to pray to any being besides Him."[48]

The adherence of halakhic man to this principle comes to the fore with particular sharpness, during the *Ne'ilah* service on the Day of Atonement. At that climactic moment of the day when the setting sun has reached the treetops and the community of Israel, lovesick and suffused with longing, feels the embrace of her Beloved and pours out her heart in psalms and hymns of praise "for the thirteen attributes [of mercy] and for the gate of tears, for it is not locked," many great Jewish scholars skipped the lovely stanza in the piyyut *Ezkerah Elohim* ["When I remember this, O God"]: "Divine attribute of mercy, intercede for us! Present our supplication before the Lord . . . for each heart is sick, each head is ailing."[49] The Halakhah views this prayer and other similar prayers as a deviation from legitimate halakhic prayer, which is fundamentally exoteric in nature. This exoteric approach is also the reason why many great halakhic scholars disapproved of the cult of the *tzaddik* in the Hasidic world. These great halakhic men had no sympathy for any practice which, in their opinion, contradicted such a fundamental halakhic principle as religious exoterism.

If you desire an exoteric, democratic religiosity, get thee unto the empirical, earthly life, the life of the body with all its two hundred forty-eight organs and three hundred sixty-five sinews. Do not turn your attention to an exalted, spiritual life rooted in abstract worlds. From the perspective of halakhic man, it is not the spirit that is charged with carrying out the religious process but the physical-biological individual, the conative individual who is led astray by the promptings of his *yetzer* and attracted to bodily pleasures.

Consequently, the Halakhah reversed the spiritual direction of *homo religiosus*. Instead of yearning to rise from below to above, from earth to heaven, from the images and shadows of reality to the plenitude of a lofty existence, to a pure ontic overflow (like the aspiration of the Platonists to the ideas, or the Neoplatonists to higher worlds that emanate from the absolutely unknowable and transcendent One), the Halakhah occupies itself with the lower realms. When halakhic man pines for God, he does not venture to rise up to Him but rather strives to bring down His divine presence into the midst of our concrete world. "One verse says: 'that I have talked with you from heaven' (Exod. 20:19) and another verse says: 'And the Lord came down upon Mount Sinai' (Exod. 19:20). How can both these verses be maintained? . . . R. Akiba says: Scripture teaches that the Holy One, blessed be He, bent down the heavens, lowering them to the top of the mountain. Rabbi says: Scripture thus teaches that the Holy One, blessed be He, bent down the lower heavens and the upper heaven of heavens, lowering them to the top of the mountain" [for R. Akiba's statement, see Mekhilta, Mesekhta de-ba-Ḥodesh, parshah 9 (on Exod. 20:19); for Rabbi's statement, ibid., parshah 4 (on Exod. 19:20)].

Homo religiosus, who thirsts for the living God, demolishes the bounds of this-worldliness, transforms himself into pure spirit, breaks through all barriers, and ascends on high. For him the approach to God consists in a leap from the empirical and concrete into the transcendent and the mysterious. Not so for halakhic man! When his soul yearns for God, he immerses himself in reality, plunges, with his entire being, into the very midst of concrete existence, and petitions God to descend upon the mountain and to dwell within our reality, with all its laws and principles. Homo religiosus ascends to God; God, however, descends to halakhic man. The latter desires not to transform finitude into infinity but rather infinity into finitude. He brings down the divine presence into a sanctuary bounded by twenty boards, holiness into a world situated within the realms of concrete reality, the Absolute into the relative and conditional. Transcendence becomes embodied in man's deeds, deeds that are shaped by the lawful physical order of which man is a part. The idea of holiness according to the halakhic world view does not signify a transcendent realm completely separate and removed from reality.[50] Similarly, it does not denote the complete actualization of the ethical ideal, of the supreme good, which is not grounded in a transcendent realm but in the domain of norms and values.[51] Holiness, according to the outlook of Halakhah, denotes the appearance of a mysterious transcendence in the midst of our concrete world, the "descent" of God, whom no thought can grasp, onto Mount Sinai, the bending down of a hidden and concealed world and lowering it onto the face of reality.

Holiness does not wink at us from "beyond" like some mysterious star that sparkles in the distant heavens, but appears in our actual, very real lives. "And one called to another and said: Holy, holy, holy is the Lord of hosts; the whole earth is full of His glory. They received one from another and said: Holy in the highest heavens, His divine abode; holy upon the earth, the work of His might; holy forever and to all eternity" (Isa. 6:3 and Targum ad loc.). The beginnings of holiness are rooted in the highest heavens, and its end is embedded in the eschatological vision of "the end of days"—holy forever and to all eternity. But the link that joins together these two perspectives is the halakhic conception of holiness: holy upon the earth, the work of His might—the holiness of the concrete. An individual does not become holy through mystical adhesion to the absolute nor through mysterious union with the infinite, nor through a boundless, all-embracing ecstasy, but, rather, through his whole biological life, through his animal actions, and through actualizing the Halakhah in the empirical world. "Speak unto all the congregation of the children of Israel . . . Ye shall be holy; for I the Lord your God am holy. . . . Ye shall fear every man his mother and his father, and ye shall keep My Sabbaths, etc. And the man that committeth adultery with another man's wife, etc. And ye shall separate between the clean beast and the unclean, and between the unclean fowl and the clean, etc. And ye shall be holy unto Me; for I the Lord am holy," etc. (Lev. 19–20). Holiness consists of a life ordered and fixed in accordance with Halakhah and finds its fulfillment

in the observance of the laws regulating human biological existence, such as the laws concerning forbidden sexual relations, forbidden foods, and similar precepts. And it was not for naught that
Maimonides included these prohibitions in his *Book of Holiness*.

Holiness is created by man, by flesh and blood.[52] Through
the power of our mouths, through verbal sanctification alone,
we can create holy offerings for the Temple treasury and
holy offerings for the altar. The land of Israel became
holy through conquest, Jerusalem, and the Temple courts—
through bringing two loaves of thanksgiving (Jerusalem)
or the remainder of the meal offering (Temple court) and
song, etc. [see Maimonides, *Laws of the Sanctuary* 6:11–16]. It is
man who sanctifies space and makes a sanctuary for his Creator.
"When God said to Moses: 'And let them make Me a sanctuary'
(Exod. 25:8), Moses began to wonder, and he said: 'The glory
of the Holy One, blessed be He, fills the upper worlds and the
lower worlds and yet He says: And let them make Me a sanctuary.' And moreover he gazed [into the future] and saw
Solomon upon the completion of the building of the Temple,
which was larger than the sanctuary, saying to the Holy One,
blessed be He: 'But will God in very truth dwell on the earth?
Behold, heaven and the heaven of heavens cannot contain
Thee; how much less this house that I have builded' (1 Kings
8:27). Therefore, Moses began to compose the psalm 'The
Most High dwelleth in concealment; the Almighty abideth in
deep darkness' (Ps. 91). God replied: 'I am not of the same
opinion as you. But twenty boards in the north and twenty in
the south and eight in the west [will suffice]. And more than
that, I will contract My divine presence [so that it may dwell] in
one square cubit'" [Exod. Rabbah 34:1]. Moses wondered:
How is it possible to bring down infinity into the midst of
finitude? How is it possible to cause the absolutely transcendent, the Most High who dwells in concealment, the Almighty
who abides in the deep darkness to reside in the midst of a
small, narrow sanctuary, in the midst of the concrete world

that is delimited by physical laws and the bounds of space and time? This problem found its expression in the question of Solomon: "But will God in very truth dwell on the earth?"— i.e., if a person pines for God, if his lovesick soul craves for her beloved and Creator, then it would appear incumbent upon him to extricate himself from the fetters of his physical being and to ascend the abstract and transcendent mountain of the Lord, for how can the physical-biological individual stand within His holy place? And yet here the standard is reversed, and we bring the glory of God down into the lower world, into the very midst of the sense realm, into the midst of space and time, into the domain of quantitative measurement. "Behold, heaven and the heaven of heavens cannot contain Thee; how much less this house that I have builded"—how can finitude contain infinity? However God's answer is: "I am not of the same opinion as you. But twenty boards in the north and twenty in the south and eight in the west. And more than that, I will contract My divine presence in one square cubit."[53]

Infinity contracts itself; eternity concentrates itself in the fleeting and transient, the Divine Presence in dimensions and the glory of God in measurements. It is Judaism that has given the world the secret of *tzimtzum*, of "contraction," contraction of the infinite within the finite, the transcendent within the concrete, the supernal within the empirical, and the divine within the realm of reality. When the Holy One, blessed be He, descended on Mount Sinai, He set an eternally binding precedent that it is God who descends to man, not man who ascends to God. When He said to Moses, "And let them make Me a sanctuary, that I may dwell among them" (Exod. 25:8), He thereby revealed the awesome mystery that God contracts His divine presence in this world.

IX

THIS mystery of *tzimtzum*, of "contraction," in the Halakhah does not touch upon questions of cosmogony. Unlike the kabbalists and (*mutatis mutandis*) Philo, Plotinus, the Neo-platonists, and the Renaissance philosophers, the Halakhah does not concern itself with metaphysical mysteries. Nor does it inquire into that which is too remote for it regarding the creation of the universe. The law of Halakhah is a practical-utilitarian one. Therefore, one should not compare the concept of *tzimtzum* in the Halakhah with the concept as it appears in mystical doctrine. There (in mystical doctrine) this idea expresses a metaphysical system that penetrates into the hidden recesses of creation, that contemplates the foundation stones of the cosmos, being and nothingness, the beginning and the end; here (in the Halakhah) the concept of *tzimtzum* does not pertain to the secrets of creation and the chariot but rather to law and judgment. Therefore, halakhic man's ontological outlook differs radically from that of the mystic. Their different interpretations of the concept of *tzimtzum* give rise to major divergences in their respective ontological stances.[54]

The mystic sees the existence of the world as a type of "affront," heaven forbid, to God's glory; the cosmos, as it were, impinges upon the infinity of the Creator. The Kabbalah senses and empathizes with the anguish of *Shekhinta be-galuta,* the Divine Presence in exile—the glory of God that emerged from the hiddenness of infinity, that became embodied in the creation of the cosmos, and that became contracted in it and by it. The creation of the world constitutes a type of "waiver" on the part of God of His own glory, "for He is holy and separate from all the worlds, and no thought can grasp Him."[55] The cosmos is a revelation of God's grace, "for His *Shekhinah,* His Divine Presence, clothes herself with worlds in order to give them life and impart existence to them."[56] Here we have revealed an awesome, mysterious antinomy that bespeaks secrets and enigmas. On the one hand, the glory of God, the most hidden, most primordial of all beings, separate, exalted, and lofty, negates all other independently existing reality, destroys and demolishes any world, be it revealed or concealed, that claims ontic status, and obliterates worlds even before the very thought of creating them arose; and on the other hand, the infinite glory contracted itself in the secret of its unity, created the world, "and clothed itself with worlds," and from this perspective it gives life to and sustains existence, "for the existence of everything is dependent upon Him."[57] The creation of the world took place on account of God's goodness, for He descended, as it were, from absolute transcendence to the domain of concrete existence and inflicted a "blemish" upon His great and awesome glory that negates all reality even before it was created. This act of creation is a "descent" for the glorious name of the Holy One, blessed be He, and the very "attribute" predicated of God, God of the world, inflicts a blemish, heaven forbid, upon the idea of the infinite, for indeed there is no existence apart from Him.[58] The very grammatical form of "God of the world"—i.e., the genitive case—is a self-contradiction, a veritable coincidence of opposites. The world cannot exist when it is directly related to God. When God's splendid majesty shines forth and stands revealed, then everything reverts to chaos and the void. Therefore, mystical doctrine contemplates existence from a pessimistic perspective, and the ontological ideal is not its ultimate end. It senses and empathizes with the anguish of the *Shekhinah*,[59] of the Divine Presence, and longs to rise up together with her from the narrow straits of reality and to cleave to the most high God "who is exalted, lofty, and separate, all alone and not manifest in any other being." This, according to mystical teaching, is the glorious and exalted eschatological vision: "In that day shall the Lord be One, and His name One" (Zech. 14:9). And every day the mystic prays for the fulfillment of this aspiration as he recites before the performance of a commandment, "I am ready and prepared to carry out the commandment of my Creator for the sake of unifying the Holy One, blessed be He, with His *Shekhinah,* with His Divine Presence."

The Holy One, blessed be He, wished to do good and, therefore, created the world. However, the world exists only from one vantage point—from the perspective of God as He who fills all worlds, or even from the viewpoint of God as He who encompasses all worlds, but not from the perspective of "God who is supreme, exceedingly lofty, exalted and uplifted," for set against Him "all worlds are nullified and they are as if they had not been and they revert to nothingness and naught."[60] Existence and naught, being and nothingness—against the perception of ontological metaphysics—do not constitute two mutually exclusive ideas but, rather, one coin on one side of which is imprinted the image of existence and on the other side that of nothingness and naught. God, qua He who fills all worlds and He who encompasses all worlds, sustains the world; qua *Deus Absconditus,* the most hidden One, He who is above and beyond the mysterious, God nullifies the world and returns it to chaos and the void. The absolute contradiction between existence and naught are only two faces that reveal themselves, as determined by the relationship between God and His creatures.[61] The desire of mystical doctrine is to free both man and the *Shekhinah,* the Divine Presence, from the world and from the visible reality which is imprinted with the stamp of the supernal.[62]

Halakhic man does not chafe against existence; rather he reads with the simplicity and innocence that is typical of him, the verse in Genesis, "And God saw everything that He had made, and, behold it was very good" (Gen. 1:31), and accepts its verdict. He does not wish to free himself from the world, and he knows nothing about the idea of the *Shekhinta be-galuta,* of the Divine Presence in exile, if taken to mean that the Divine

Presence is held captive in the tresses of the cosmos and the
chains of reality. He is completely suffused with an unqualified
ontological optimism and is totally immersed in the cosmos.
On the contrary, as he sees it, the task of man is to bring down
the Divine Presence to the lower world, to this vale of tears.
The mystery of *tzimtzum* should not precipitate metaphysical
anguish but rather gladness and joy. Man resides together with
his Creator in this world, and it is only through cultivating that
togetherness in the here and now that man can acquire a share
in the world to come. The creation of the world does not inflict
any "blemish" upon the idea of divinity, does not infringe
upon infinity; on the contrary, it is the will of God that His
Shekhinah, His Divine Presence, should contract and limit itself
within the realm of empirical reality. The great promised
destiny, "In that day shall the Lord be one, and His name one"
(Zech. 14:9), instead of referring to the mystical dream of the
overcoming and negation of reality, refers to the era in which
the Halakhah will find its fulfillment, its total realization in this
world. The creation of the world is, in essence, the revelation
of the will of God and is not a manifestation of His goodness
and grace.

R. Simha Zelig, the disciple and friend of R. Hayyim, related to me the following incident: Once he and R. Hayyim
visited someone's house in Vilna. While they were waiting for
their host to appear, R. Hayyim glanced through some works of
Habad Hasidism that were lying on the table. The books apparently discussed the question of God's motivation in creating
the world and cited two opinions: (1) God created the world for
the sake of His goodness; (2) He created it for the sake of His
grace. R Hayyim turned to R. Simha Zelig and with utter seriousness told him: "Both views are incorrect, the world was
created neither for the sake of His goodness, nor for the sake
of His grace but for the sake of His will." This view, set down by
Maimonides as a firm principle in the *Guide*[63] and prevalent in
many forms in voluntaristic religious and metaphysical sys-

tems—e.g., that of Solomon ibn Gabirol in *Mekor hayyim* [Fountain of life] and that of Duns Scotus (who was influenced by the former)—is the very seal of halakhic man.[64] The world was created in accordance with the will of God, who wills to contract His Divine Presence in it.[65] Therefore, we are called to act and to arrange our lives in accordance with this fundamental idea.

While the mystic shares in the anguish of *Shekhinta be-galuta*, of the Divine Presence in exile, the Divine Presence of "God who conceals Himself in His dazzling Hiddenness," "lofty and exalted, abiding in the heavens" [from a piyyut recited on the High Holidays], that descended into the midst of the cosmos,[66] halakhic man declares that the true home of the Divine Presence is in this world. The Divine Presence goes into exile, according to the opinion of halakhic man, when it departs from this world to the hidden and awesome transcendental realm. "The Divine Presence left Israel by ten stages—this we know from reference in the Scripture: [it went] from ark cover to the holy cherub. . . . And from the wilderness it ascended and settled in its [exalted and remote, transcendent] place as it is written, 'I will go and return to My place' (Hosea 5:15)."[67] When the Divine Presence returns to its original place, when it rises to transcendence, to the heights of the heavens, there to conceal itself in the shadow of absolute separateness and complete estrangement from this world, the Temple is destroyed and the long chapter of the exile of the Divine Presence begins. The ideal of halakhic man is that the Divine Presence should rest here in this world. "And there I will meet with thee, and I will speak with thee from above the ark-cover" (Exod. 25:22). This verse represents the ultimate telos of the Halakhah. "R. Aba bar Kahana said: It is not written in the text 'And they heard the voice of the Lord God walking [*mehalekh: pi'el* form] in the garden' but 'And they heard the voice of the Lord God skipping [*mithalekh: hitpa'el* form] in the garden' (Gen. 3:8). This [use of the reflexive] implies that He sprang ever upward [i.e., they heard God *departing* from the garden]. The principle abode of the Divine Presence was in the lower realms. As soon as Adam sinned, the Divine Presence betook itself to the first firmament; Cain sinned, it betook itself to the second firmament; the generation of Enosh to the third; the generation of the flood to the fourth; the generation of dispersion to the fifth; the Sodomites to the sixth; the Egyptians in the time of Abraham to the seventh. As a counterpart to these there arose seven righteous men who brought down the Divine Presence from above to below. Abraham arose and brought it down to the sixth firmament . . . and Moses arose and brought it down from above [the first firmament] to below [the earth]. Rabbi Isaac said: It is written: 'The righteous shall inherit the land and dwell therein forever' (Ps. 37:29). What then shall the wicked do? Shall they fly about in the air? The meaning rather is that the wicked did not cause the Divine Presence to dwell upon the earth, but the righteous did cause the Divine Presence to dwell upon the earth."[68] "R. Huna said: The Torah teaches you a rule of etiquette: the bridegroom should not enter the bridal chamber until the bride gives him permission. Hence it is written: 'Let my beloved come into his garden' (Songs 4:16) and [only] afterward [does the bridegroom state] 'I am come into My garden' (Songs 5:1). R. Azariah in the name of R. Judah b. R. Simon said: To what may the matter be compared? To a king who was angry with his wife and drove her away and expelled her from his palace. After a while he sought to recall her. She said: Let him give me some new token and then recall me. Similarly in times past Adam dwelt in the garden of Eden in the company of the Divine Presence. The Holy One, blessed be He, was angry with him and drove him from His private territory. When Israel went out of Egypt, the Holy One, blessed be He, wished to restore them to His own immediate vicinity and told them to make for Him a sanctuary, as it is written: 'And let them make Me a sanctuary' (Exod. 25:8). Said Israel: Let the Holy One, blessed be He, give us some new token that He wishes to restore us to Himself. What

was the new token? In former times the Holy One, blessed be
He, used to receive sacrifices on high, as it is written: 'And the
Lord smelled the sweet savor' (Gen. 8:21). But from now on He
will receive sacrifices from below. Hence it is written: 'Let my
beloved come into his garden'—this is the Divine Presence—
'and eat his precious fruits'—these are the sacrifices. R. Ishmael b. R. Jose said: It does not say in the text 'I am come into
the garden,' but 'I am come into My garden.' This means into
My bridal chamber—namely, into the place which has been My
principle abode from the very beginning, for the principle
abode of the Divine Presence is in the lower realms."[69]

Because of man's sins, the Divine Presence betook itself on
high and the chosen of all human beings, Moses our teacher,
brought it down below. The garden of God is this world, not a
supernal one.

Halakhic man resembles somewhat the mathematician who
masters infinity only for the sake of creating finitude, delimited
by numbers and mathematical measures, and cognizing it. The
Halakhah, from the perspective of the process of contraction,
also uses the method of quantification; it quantifies quality and
religious subjectivity in the form of concrete, objective phenomena that are standardized and measurable. "The laws
relating to standards, interpositions, and partitions are laws
revealed to Moses on Mount Sinai" [Eruvin 4a; Sukkah 5b].
The Halakhah fixes firmly established and clearly delimited
laws, statutes, and measures for each and every commandment—what constitutes eating and what are its measurements,
what constitutes drinking and what are its standards, what
constitutes a fruit and what are its stages of development and
distinguishing characteristics, the thirty-nine categories of work
on the Sabbath and their measurements, the measurements of
a tent that defiles, partitions, units of monetary value, and
many more.

"Now because the commandments were given to us by way
of being clothed in the attribute of strength and by the contrac-

tion of the light ... therefore, most commandments have a delimited, 'contracted' measure. For instance, the length of the *tzitzit* [must be] twelve times the width of the thumb; the phylacteries, two fingers by two fingers and necessarily square; the *lulav*, four handbreaths; the *sukkah*, seven handbreaths; the *shofar*, one handbreath; the *mikvah*, forty se'ahs. Similarly, the sacrifices have a delimited, 'contracted' measure as regards age, as, for instance, 'lambs of the first year' (Exod. 29:38). . . . And similarly, the act of charity and the performance of deeds of lovingkindness with one's money, even though it is one of the pillars upon which the world stands, and as it is written 'The world was built by *ḥesed*, lovingkindness' (Ps. 89:3), nevertheless it has a fixed measure: one who wishes to perform the commandment of charity in the most perfect manner must give one-fifth, while for one who wishes to fulfill the commandment in an ordinary manner, one-tenth suffices. For since the world is delimited and measured ... the Torah's commandments of charity and deeds of lovingkindness were also given a measure and standard just like the other commandments."[70] R. Shneur Zalman of Lyady, the founder of Habad Hasidism, that great luminary of Halakhah and mysticism, sensed that the fundamental method of the Halakhah is that act of quantification which is so integral a part of the mystery of *tzimtzum*. This wondrous principle expresses itself in two parallel dimensions: in the real world—in empirical reality—and in the ideal world—in halakhic constructions. The supernal will clothes itself in these two creations and becomes embodied through them in the attribute of strength (*gevurah*) and contraction, from whose midst there flows the method of quantification. Moreover, "God hath set the one against the other" (Eccles. 7:14): God has introduced a parallelism; for just as the qualitative reality to which our senses are exposed lends itself to quantification by cognitive man, who turns qualities into quantities, percepts into equations, so, too, the supernal illumination, "which may be perceived by means of the many mighty contractions which it undergoes as the different levels [of reality] emanate from one another," is placed within and under the dominion of the delimited, "contracted," quantitative act. The "movement" from quality to quantity, from experience to equations, which takes place in the real, empirical world, also finds its expression in the ideal realm of Halakhah.

The statement of Galileo that "the great book which ever lies before our eyes—I mean the Universe—is written in mathematical language and the characters are triangles, circles, and other geometrical figures" applies as well to the Halakhah. And not for naught did the Gaon of Vilna tell the translator of Euclid's geometry into Hebrew [R. Barukh of Shklov], that "To the degree that a man is lacking in the wisdom of mathematics he will lack one hundredfold in the wisdom of the Torah." This statement is not just a pretty rhetorical conceit that testifies to the broad-mindedness of the Gaon but a firmly established truth of halakhic epistemology. The fundamental tendency of the Halakhah is to translate the qualitative features of religious subjectivity—the content of religious man's consciousness, which surges and swells like the waves of the sea, then pounds against the shore of reality, there to shatter and break—into firm and well-established quantities "like nails well fastened" (Eccles. 12:11) that no storm can uproot from their place. The supernal will is reflected both in the mirror of reality and the mirror of the ideal Halakhah, through the medium of objective, quantitative measurements.[71]

A subjective religiosity cannot endure. And all those tendencies to transform the religious act into pure subjectivity negate all corporeality and all sensation in religious life and admit man into a pure and abstract world, where there is neither eating nor drinking, but religious individuals sitting with their crowns on their heads and enjoying their own inner experiences, their own tempestuous, heaven-storming spirits their own hidden longings and mysterious yearnings—will in the end prove null and void. The stychic power of religion that seizes hold of man, that subjects and dominates him, is in force only when the religion is a concrete religion, a religion of the life of the senses, in which there is sight, smell, and touch, a religion which a man of flesh and blood can feel with all of his senses, sinews, and organs, with his entire being, a sensuous religion which conative man will encounter, in a very palpable way, wherever he may go. A subjective religiosity comprised of spiritual moods, of emotions and affections, of outlooks and desires, will never be blessed with success.

Halakhic man never accepted the ruling of Maimonides opposing the recital of piyyutim, the liturgical poems and songs of praise. Go forth and learn what the *Guide* sought to do to the piyyutim of Israel! "Thus what we do [in prayer] is not like what is done by the truly ignorant who spoke at great length and spent great efforts on prayers that they composed and on sermons that they compiled. . . . In these prayers and sermons they predicate of God qualitative attributions that, if predicated of a human individual, would designate a deficiency in him. . . . This kind of license is frequently taken by poets and preachers or such as think what they speak is poetry, so that the utterances of some . . . contain rubbish and perverse imaginings."[72] Nevertheless, on the High Holidays the community of Israel, singing the hymns of unity and glory, reaches out to its Creator. And when the Divine Presence winks at us from behind the fading rays of the setting sun and its smile bears within it forgiveness and pardon, we weave a "royal crown" of praise for the *Atik Yomin,* the Ancient One. And in moments of divine mercy and grace, in times of spiritual ecstasy and exaltation, when our entire existence thirsts for the living God, we recite many piyyutim and hymns, and we disregard the strictures of the philosophical midrash concerning the problem of negative attributes. The Halakhah does not deem it necessary to reckon with speculative concepts and very fine, subtle abstractions on the one hand and vague feelings, obscure experiences, inchoate affections, and elusive subjectivity on the other. It determines law and judgment in Israel.

The Halakhah, which was given to us from Sinai, is the objectification of religion in clear and determinate forms, in precise and authoritative laws, and in definite principles. It translates subjectivity into objectivity, the amorphous flow of religious experience into a fixed pattern of lawfulness.[73] To what may the matter be compared? To the physicist who transforms light and sound and all of the contents of our qualitative perceptions into quantitative relationships, mathematical functions, and objective fields of force. In the same manner as many philosophical schools accepted the position of Plato and Aristotle that existence means fixity, regularity, and orderliness, so the Halakhah declares that any religiosity which does not lead to determinate actions, firm and clear-cut measures, chiseled and delimited laws and statutes will prove sterile. The concept of nonbeing or of hylic matter also exists in the world of religion. Experience has shown that the whole religious ideology which bases itself on the subjective nature of religion— from Schleiermacher and Kierkegaard to Natorp—can have dangerous, destructive consequences that far outweigh any putative gains.

The Halakhah wishes to objectify religiosity not only through introducing the external act and the psychophysical deed into the world of religion but also through the structuring and ordering of the inner correlative in the realm of man's spirit. The Halakhah sets down statutes and erects markers that serve as a dam against the surging, subjective current coursing through the universal *homo religiosus*, which, from time to time, in its raging turbulence sweeps away his entire being to obscure and inchoate realms. Indeed, many halakhic authorities have even sanctioned, after the fact, a mechanical performance of a commandment, one lacking in intention.[74] (Only the intention not to discharge one's obligation would invalidate the performance of the commandment.) And even according to those authorities who declare that commandments do require intention, the Halakhah does not require of us any mystical, esoteric intentions directed toward a *mundus absconditus,* a hidden world, but only the clear, plain thought to fulfill via this particular act such and such a commandment. Heaps upon heaps of mystical intentions and unifications have been piled up by the mystics to lead man's consciousness to hidden worlds; halakhic man knows nothing, however, about such mysteries. The intention accompanying the performance of a commandment appears in the Halakhah illumined by the light of objectivity and lawfulness. Both the intention and the deed are part of the process of objectification. "As to the view that an individual, before he performs a commandment, must state that he is performing it with a mystical intention . . . we see that such mystical intentions, whether they accompany prayer or the commandments, often involve perverse and wayward notions and indeed border on the heretical, as has been clearly demonstrated. Certainly, therefore, we should wholly abolish reciting mystical intentions. And it suffices to perform the commandment for the sake of the commandment. . . . And any commandment which is not preceded by a blessing, my practice is to recite beforehand 'I am performing this action in order to fulfill the comandment of my Creator.' And this alone suffices, and nothing more is needed. And the intention [required for prayer] is simply understanding the meaning of the words."[75] All great halakhic scholars have acted in accordance with this decision.

Once my father was standing on the synagogue platform on Rosh Ha-Shanah, ready and prepared to guide the order of the sounding of the *shofar.* The *shofar*-sounder, a god-fearing Habad Hasid who was very knowledgeable in the mystical doctrine of the "Alter Rebbe," R. Shneur Zalman of Lyady, began to weep. My father turned to him and said: "Do you weep when you take the *lulav?* Why then do you weep when

you sound the *shofar*? Are not both commandments of God?"
The mystic understands the symbolic significance of the sounding of the *shofar*—the concept of a plain note—whereby man
attempts to pierce through lawful existence and reach the
throne of glory of the *Atik Yomin*, the Ancient One, the *Deus
Absconditus*. The sounding of the *shofar*, according to the outlook of R. Shneur Zalman, expresses the powerful aspiration
of *homo religiosus* to extricate himself from the straits of contraction—the divine realm of strength—and enter into the
wide spaces of expansion—the divine realm of grace—and
from thence to rise above the seven lower divine realms, "the
cornerstones of the [cosmic structure]" into the hidden world
in which the light of the *Ein-Sof*, the completely hidden infinite
God, gleams and shines, as it were. Man's weeping on Rosh
Ha-Shanah, according to this doctrine, is the weeping of the soul
that longs for its origin, for the rock from whence it was hewn,
that yearns to cleave to its beloved not in hiding, but openly.
The sounding of the *shofar* protests against reality and denies
the universe itself. The entire ontological pessimism of mystical doctrine can be heard from the midst of the *shofar* in its
long, drawn-out sighs and short, piercing cries [cf. Rosh Ha-
Shanah 33b–34a]. When a person takes the *shofar* and issues
forth a blast, he thereby protests against the reality that separates him from the *Ein-Sof*. He groans bitterly and moans over
his inability to leap over the mountains of being that divide his
soul from its Creator. The *shofar* heralds the great and awesome [eschatological] day of judgment when the Holy One,
blessed be He, will appear and fill His world with a terrible
dread. "The angels quaking with fear declare: The day of
judgment is here, to bring the hosts of heaven in judgment:
Indeed, even they are not guiltless in Thy sight in judgment"
[from the piyyut, *U-netaneh tokef*, recited in the Musaf services
on the High Holidays]. Judgment means an ontological weighing and evaluation of finite existence from the perspective of
infinity. The attribute of judgment by its nature tends to tip the

ontological scale to the side of guilt and causes existence to revert back to chaos and the void. Therefore, on Rosh Ha-Shanah a person ventures to rise up from the divine realm of strength—i.e. judgment—to the divine realm of grace and from thence to "A God dreaded in the great council of the holy ones" (Ps. 89:8), outside concrete reality. Not so the commandment of taking the *lulav* and the *etrog*, which symbolizes the longings of man for God who illumines the path of all worlds, who dwells in the midst of reality itself, and who has contracted His light, as it were, within the forms of concrete existence in all its manifestations.

The sounding of the *shofar* represents the yearning for the *Deus Absconditus* whom no thought can grasp, who is separate and removed, awesome and holy. The *shofar* weeps, wails, and moans over the infinite distance that separates the cosmos from the *Ein-Sof*, the infinite God. Therefore, it negates the world and raises man to the most absolute transcendent mode of existence. In contrast, the taking of the *lulav* and the *etrog*— the fruit of a goodly tree—sustains and affirms the beautiful and resplendent world, which reflects the glory of the God who fills and encompasses all worlds.[76]

The Targum, the Aramaic translation of the Pentateuch, translates the biblical name of Rosh Ha-Shanah, "a day of the blast" (*Yom Teruah*) (Num. 29:1), as "a day of moaning" (*Yom Yevavah*).[77] In contrast, the Torah enjoined special rejoicing on the festival of Sukkot. "And ye shall rejoice before the Lord your God seven days" (Lev. 23:40).[78] Halakhic man, however, does not distinguish between the two commandments. He is completely immersed in the cosmos whether on Rosh Ha-Shanah or Sukkot. The mystics cleave asunder the barriers of the objectivity and the concreteness of the commandment. On a wondrous craft they navigate the waves of a mysterious subjectivity that surges and flows, that is constantly changing its shape and form, that is always metamorphosing, assuming new images, different guises; and the waves come and sweep the craft along and carry them unto paradisiacal realms. Not so is the manner of halakhic man! He does not wish to snap the fetters of the objective form and demolish the iron bars of the firm and fixed lawfulness of this world. The *Shekhinah*, the Divine Presence, does not anguish over the mystery of *tzimtzum*, over her descent into the empirical realm; accordingly, halakhic man does not wish to free either her or himself from this realm.

X

HALAKHIC man's relationship to existence is not only ontological but also normative in nature. In truth, the ontological approach serves as the vestibule whence he may enter the banquet-hall of normative understanding [cf. Avot 4:21]. Halakhic man cognizes the world in order to subordinate it to religious performances. For instance, he cognizes space by means of religious, a priori, lawful categories in order to realize in it the halakhic norm of Sabbath, the commandment of *sukkah*, and the idea of purity. He "engages in the same type of calculations as do the astronomers" [Maimonides, *Laws of the Sanctification of the New Moon*, 1:6] in order to determine seasons and festivals. He studies the plant world for the purpose of classifying their species, as such classification relates to the laws of diverse seeds, and for the purpose of determining the standards of growth, since such determination affects the agricultural laws. Thus his normative doctrine has priority, from a teleological perspective, over his ontological approach. Cognition is for the purpose of doing. "Great is study, for study leads to action" [Kiddushin 40b]. However, even the norm is, at the outset, ideal, not real. Halakhic man is not particularly concerned about the possibility of actualizing the norm in the concrete world. He wishes to mint an ideal, normative coin. Even those laws that are not practiced in the present time are subjected to his normative viewpoint, this despite the fact that he is unable nowadays to fulfill these particular commandments. The maxim of the sages "Great is study, for study leads to action" has a twofold meaning:

1. action may mean determining the Halakhah or ideal norm;
2. action may refer to implementing the ideal norm in the real world.

Halakhic man stresses action in its first meaning. However, cognition itself is directed toward the ethos, not toward the logos. From this perspective, therefore, halakhic man resembles *homo religiosus,* not cognitive man, for while cognitive man is not norm-oriented, is not out to discover the hidden imperative in every brook and stone,[79] *homo religiosus* hears the echo of the norm forthcoming from every aspect of creation. "The heavens declare the glory of God, and the firmament reciteth His handiwork" (Ps. 19:2).

But what is the tale of the heavens, if not the proclamation of the norm? What is the recitation of the firmament if not the declaration of the commandment? All of existence declares the glory of God—man's obligation to order his life according to the will of the Almighty. The principle of "And thou shalt walk in His ways" (Deut. 28:9) (*imitatio Dei*) flows from halakhic man's normative relationship to the world. We can know God's ways only through studying the cosmos, for it is in the cosmos that there stand revealed before us the glorious and resplendent attributes of action. And, as Maimonides already taught in the *Guide* (I, 54), the cognition of the attributes of action is the source of ethical life. In order to implement the ethical ideal we must fix upon the whole of being and cognize it. This cognition is teleological in essence—it aims to reveal the traces of the norm hidden within reality.

However, while *homo religiosus* accepts the norm against his will, "as though a demon compelled him" [cf. Nedarim 20b], halakhic man does not experience any consciousness of com-

Cmdmts feel like existential truth

pulsion accompanying the norm. Rather, it seems to him as though he discovered the norm in his innermost self, as though it was not just a commandment that had been imposed upon him, but an existential law of his very being. Halakhic man does not struggle with his evil impulses, nor does he clash with the tempter who seeks to deprive him of his senses. Halakhic men are not subject to the whispered proffer of desire, and they need not exert themselves to resist its pull.

Halakhic man is firmly embedded in this world and does not suffer from the pangs of the dualism of the spiritual and the corporeal, of the soul which ascends on high and the body which descends below. We do not have here a person who strains against the chains of the ethical and the reign of the norm and accepts them against his will. Rather, we have a blending of the obligation with self-consciousness, a merging of the norm with the individual, and a union of an outside command with the inner will and conscience of man. Unlike the Christian saints whose lives consisted of a long series of battles with the dazzling allure of life, with carnal, this-worldly pleasures, the great Jewish scholars know nothing about man's conflict with the evil urge. The church fathers devoted themselves to religious life in a state of compulsion and duress, the Jewish sages, in a state of joy and freedom. Thus King David, who said, "Day unto day pours forth speech and night unto night pronounces knowledge" (Ps. 19:3), goes on in the great eightfold, alphabetical Psalm of the Law (Ps. 119) [the name ascribed to this psalm in Berakhot 4b] to say, "I will delight myself in Thy commandments, which I have loved. . . . This is my comfort in my affliction, that Thy word hath quickened me" (Ps. 119:47, 50). We do not have here a directive that imposes upon man obligations against which he rebels, but delightful commandments which his soul passionately desires. When halakhic man comes to the real world, he has already created his ideal, a priori image, which shines with the radiance of the norm. The real world does not impose upon him anything new, nor does it compel him to perform any new action of which he had not been aware beforehand in his ideal world. And this ideal world is his very own, his own possession; he is free to create in it, to arrive at new insights, to improve and perfect. Spiritual freedom and intellectual independence reign there in unlimited fashion. Consequently, it seems to him as though this ideal world is his own creation. Therefore, he is free and independent in his normative understanding. "The only free man is he who occupies himself with the Torah" [Avot 6:2]. He who occupies himself with the Torah and gleans new creative insights from it is indeed a free and independent man.[80]

XI

THIS fundamental opposition between the ontological outlooks of *homo religiosus* and halakhic man is reflected in the very being of these two personalities; it pervades their entire characters.

The tendency toward subjectivity, toward the blurring of forms and boundaries, toward the confusion of domains—the lower with the higher, the corporeal with the spiritual, the revealed with the concealed—of *homo religiosus* and the thrust toward objectivity and lawfulness, toward a firmly established creation, well formed, possessing boundaries, statutes, and judgments of halakhic man, mold the images of these two godly individuals.

Homo religiosus is indeed highly subjective. He is different from scientific man, who is distinguished by his objectivity, his psychic equilibrium, and an almost eerie indifference. When cognitive man approaches the world, he takes great care that he not be disqualified as an interested party. He is not concerned in advance with the results of his cognition and study; he is but "a watchman and scout, a scribe, recorder, and enumerator" [terms from the Musaf prayer of Rosh Ha-Shanah].

hala are not just observer, record

This is not the case with *homo religiosus*! When he stands before the cosmos, he is entirely aflame with the holy fire of wonder, he is all ashudder, confronted with the incomprehensible and unknown. His soul rages and storms like a tempestuous sea. He is frightened—nay terrified—by the mystery. He hides his face, for he is afraid to look upon it. He flees from it, but at the same time, against his will, he draws near to it; enchanted, he finds himself irresistibly pulled toward it, pines for it, and longs to merge with it. *Homo religiosus* is suspended between two giant magnets, between love and fear, between desire and dread, between longing and anxiety. He is caught between two opposing forces—the right hand of existence embraces him, the left thrusts him aside. Indeed, there is a great deal of truth in the view of Otto that fascination and repulsion constitute the two fundamental experiences of *homo religiosus*.

As a result of fluttering to and fro between these powerful opposing pulls, *homo religiosus* suffers from psychic torments and spiritual anguish. He undergoes terrible pains in the search for the enigma that will only darken reality even more, in the quest for a cognition that will only deepen the wonder, but at the same time he delights in those very pains. At times *homo religiosus* is a masochist picking away at his own wounds and reveling in his own pain. These pains contain within themselves the sweetness of eternity, a taste of the world to come. The enjoyment of pain and delight in suffering can bring him to religious ecstasy. "How beloved are my sufferings" [cf. Sanhedrin 101a], exclaims *homo religiosus* as he contemplates the struggles, the pangs of his soul and spirit. For in those very pains, those spiritual lacerations, the desire for transcendence comes to the fore.

It is in this light that we can understand the deep contradiction pervading the spiritual self-evaluation of *homo religiosus*. On the one hand, he senses his own lowliness and insignificance, his own frailty and weakness; he knows that even "a gnat preceded him, a snail preceded him."[81] He sees himself as a the one biological creature who has misused his own talents for destructive ends, who has failed in the task assigned to him.[82] On the other hand, he is aware of his own greatness and loftiness, how his spirit breaks through all barriers and ascends to the very heights, bores through all obstacles and descends to the very depths. Is he not the crown of creation to whom God granted dominion over all the work of His hands? "And God blessed them and God said unto them: 'Be fruitful and multiply, and fill the earth and subdue it, and have dominion over the fish of the sea, over the fowl of the heaven, and over the beasts and all over the earth'" (Gen. 1:28)—this is the blessing that God bestowed upon man. This antinomy is an integral part of man's creature consciousness; more, it is the source of the entire dispute concerning man's place within the cosmos,[83] from the days of the Sophists and, later on, Socrates, Plato, and Aristotle, until Nietzsche, Klages, and Scheler. The essence of the antinomy is rooted in the religious consciousness, the source of most of the antinomies and contradictions in man's outlook. From a religious perspective, man, in his relationship to the world, oscillates between the two poles of self-negation and absolute pride, between the consciousness of his nothingness and the consciousness of the infinity deep within him.[84] *Homo religiosus* can never be free of this oscillation. In the depths of his consciousness he is entangled in the thicket of two contradictory verses. One verse declares, "When I behold Thy heavens, the work of Thy fingers, the moon and the stars which Thou hast established; what is man, that Thou art mindful of him, and the son of man, that Thou thinkest of him?" (Ps. 8:4–5), while the other verse declares, "Yet Thou hast made him but a little lower than the angels, and hast crowned him with glory and honor. Thou hast made him to have dominion over the works of Thy hands; Thou hast put all things under his feet" (Ps. 8:6–7). And *homo religiosus* has yet to find the third harmonizing verse.

However, halakhic man *has* found the third verse—the

Halakhah. He, too, suffers from this dualism, from this deep
spiritual split, but he mends the split through the concept of
Halakhah and law.

Halakhic man also stands on the Day of Atonement, as the
sun is setting, as that great and holy day sinks into the fiery sea
of glory and eternity, and, in the climactic *Ne'ilah* prayer,
confesses his sins before his Creator. He begins: "What are we?
What is our life? What is our goodness? What is our virtue?
What our help? What our strength? What our might? What
can we say to Thee, Lord our God and God of our fathers?
Indeed, all heroes are as nothing in Thy sight, the men of
renown as though they never existed, the wise as though they
lacked knowledge, the intelligent as though they lacked insight; for most of their actions are worthless, the days of their
lives are vanity in Thy presence: 'so that man hath no pre-
eminence above a beast; for all is vanity' (Eccles. 3:19)." And, in
truth, what is man when set against the vast universe and the
heavenly realms? What is his worth in comparison to the cosmic
process? What is he when set against the world and the fullness
thereof? What is he in relation to worlds, visible and invisible?
And the first verse comes and gnaws away at him: "When I
behold Thy heavens, the work of Thy fingers, the moon and
the stars which Thou hast established; what is man, that Thou
art mindful of him, and the son of man, that Thou thinkest of
him?" And a deep, hidden anxiety seizes hold of him; a great
dread springs upon him and nullifies his being and selfhood. He
is overcome by despair; filled with loathing and self-contempt.
However, at that very moment one thought flashes through his
mind. If "man hath no pre-eminence above a beast; for all is
vanity," then what is the nature of the Day of Atonement?
What is the meaning of pardon and forgiveness? What is the
purpose of the sacrificial service of the day, the private, intimate encounter between the high priest and his Creator in the
holy of holies? What is the whole nature of the holiness of the
day, that holiness which bestows atonement upon us? Why

should we be confronted at all with the concept of sin and iniquity on the one side and the obligation to repent on the other? Indeed, the Halakhah set man at the very center of its world, and the Day of Atonement testifies to this. And if this is so, how can the first verse be maintained? And straightaway man is filled with a longing and yearning for God that undergirds and upholds his position in the world. Behold, my very existence bears witness to my worth! Indeed, I am the one creature in this world who reflects the image of Divine Presence. Do I not study the Torah, the cherished plaything [see Ps. 119:77] of the Holy One, blessed be He? The angels themselves long to learn Torah from me! Am I not at this very moment reaching out to my lover and beloved? Halakhic man immediately discovers his redemption and the endorsement of his existence in this awareness and begins: "Thou hast chosen man at the very inception and Thou hast recognized him as worthy of standing before Thee." In a single moment his stature is so enhanced that he feels he can touch the very heavens! In the blinking of an eye the lowliest of creatures turns into the noblest of creatures, whom the Holy One, blessed be He, elected at the very inception and recognized as worthy of standing before Him. *Standing before God!* What self-esteem is present here! What majesty and strength engirdles halakhic man when he utters this phrase! What might lies hidden deep within these three words! Man stands before God, and the *Atik Yomin,* the Ancient One, Himself approves of man's being and existence.

The mystics argue that when finitude confronts infinity, everything reverts to chaos and the void; in their view all existence has come into being only by virtue of the mystery of *tzimtzum,* of "contraction"—i.e., the concealment of the glory and light of God. Hence, for them, "before God" means the disappearance of the world. Halakhic man, however, declares that "contraction" does not consist in God's concealing His face but rather in His revealing His glory. Man finds his existence to be full, rich, and holy even when standing before the Infinite one; and the *Deus Absconditus* does not, heaven forbid, negate its value and reality. And let the Halakhah itself be proof! God commanded man, and the very command itself carries with it the endorsement of man's existence. If man, when confronted by God, would revert to nothingness and naught, then the command, which is the very foundation of the Halakhah, would be incomprehensible. For certainly God would not make a mockery of His Torah! The fact that God linked Himself with man and prescribed for him laws, statutes, and judgments bears witness that He, may He be blessed, does not nullify and obliterate man's being. And, while the setting sun is still shedding a brilliant light, halakhic man continues his prayer: "And Thou hast given unto us, O Lord our God, with love this Day of Atonement, the climax of pardon and forgiveness for all our sins in order that we cease from the oppression of our hands and return unto Thee to perform with a whole heart the statutes which Thou hast willed." The Day of Atonement which was given unto us in love, the promise of pardon and forgiveness, the obligation to repent, the existence of the statutes which God has willed are the clearest and strongest testimony to man's importance, his central place in the world. The second verse contradicts the first: "Yet Thou hast made him but a little lower than the angels, and hast crowned him with glory and honor," etc. The Halakhah serves as the third harmonizing verse. The man who does not live according to the Halakhah and who does not participate in the realization of the ideal world is of no worth. "Before I was formed I was of no worth, and now that I have been formed it is as if I have not been formed. Dust I am in my life, and all the more so in death" [conclusion of the *Ne'ilah* prayer]. However, the man who knows his duty, his task as a partner in the creation of worlds through constructing a halakhic world and actualizing it in reality has been elected by God at the very inception and has been recognized as worthy of standing before Him. "It were better for man not to have been created than to have been created, but now that he has been created, let him examine his [past] deeds. This is the authoritative halakhic judgment of the sages, and it means that *repentance* harmonizes the two verses.[85]

XII

EVEN though this mode of consciousness on the part of halakhic man is impaired at times, for he, too, in part draws upon the same psychic sources as does *homo religiosus*, it nevertheless molds and fashions his spiritual makeup. Halakhic man knows no fear or dread in the full sense of the term. When he approaches the world, he is armed with his weapons—i.e., his laws—and the consciousness of lawfulness and order that is implanted within him serves to ward off the fear that springs upon him. Halakhic man does not enter a strange, alien, mysterious world, but a world with which he is already familiar through the a priori which he carries within his consciousness. He enters into the real world via the ideal creation which in the end will be actualized—in whole or in part—in concrete reality, and there exists between the two a relationship of analogy. Why, then, should he be afraid? Such concepts as nothingness and naught, chaos and the void, darkness and the abyss are wholly foreign to him. His entire world is "builded with turrets" (Songs 4:4), layer upon layer, and he, halakhic man, may be compared to the honor guard which surrounds the palace of the king, "where the watch is only for the sake of its glory" [Maimonides, *Laws of the Sanctuary* 8:1]. Nothingness lies not in wait for him, nor does the naught peer out of the latticework of existence. Halakhic man does not give any thought to the "other side," that *tertium quid* of being and nothingness. He is unfamiliar with the dark back streets of defilement, nor does he ever go astray in the blind alleys and narrow pathways of the world's emptiness and chaos. All stands before him, beautiful, finished, and adorned. Halakhic man is a man of the law and the principle, a man of the statute and the judgment, and, therefore, he always possesses in his being, even if at times it should be afflicted with a deep melancholy, a fixed, firm, Archimedean point that is outside and above the turbulence of his soul, beyond the maelstrom of the affective life, a true source of peace and tranquillity. Halakhic man vanquishes even the fear of death, which, as was explained above, is rooted in his world perspective, by means of the law and the Halakhah, and he transforms the phenomenon, which so terrifies him, into an object of man's observation and cognition. For when death becomes an object of man's cognition, the fright accompanying death dissipates. Death is frightening, death is menacing, death is dreadful only so long as it appears as a subject confronting man. However, when man succeeds in transforming death-subject into death-object, the horror is gone. My father related to me that when the fear of death would seize hold of R. Hayyim, he would throw himself, with his entire heart and mind, into the study of the laws of tents and corpse defilement. And these laws, which revolve about such difficult and complex problems as defilement of a grave, defilement of a tent, blocked-up defilement, interposition before defilement, a vessel with a tight fitting cover upon it in a tent in which a corpse lies, etc., etc., would calm the turbulence of his soul and would imbue it with a spirit of joy and gladness. When halakhic man fears death, his sole weapon wherewith to fight this terrible dread is the eternal law of the Halakhah. The act of objectification triumphs over the subjective terror of death.[86] The mysterious relationship in effect between the cognizing subject and the object that is comprehended, even though it is logical and not psychological, results in any event in man deeming himself lord and master with respect to the thing that is about to be comprehended. The subject rules over the object, the person over the thing. Knowledge, by definition, is the subjugation of the object and the domination of the subject.[87]

thru cognition are overcome,

Therefore, if a person is afraid of a particular phenomenon, let him approach it with the standard of cognition, and then he shall be delivered from dread and terror. It is through cognition that he "acquires" the object that strikes such alarm into him; he brings it into his domain and obtains title to it. The terrifying abyss disappears, the strangeness fades from sight and leaves no trace behind. A warm and cordial relationship wells up. The enemy becomes a friend, the foe a familiar acquaintance.

It would seem to me that this world perspective was the primary factor in the refusal on the part of such halakhic men as R. Hayyim of Brisk, R. Naftali Zevi Yehudah Berlin of Volozhin, and such like to admit the Musar program of R. Israel Salanter into the yeshivah of Volozhin. This movement, at the beginning of its growth, symbolized the world perspective of the universal *homo religiosus,* a perspective directed toward the transcendent, toward that existence lying beyond the realm of concrete reality. The emotion of fear, the sense of lowliness, the melancholy so typical of *homo religiosus,*[88] self-negation, constant self-appraisal, the consciousness of sin, self-lacerating torments, etc., etc., constituted the primary features of the movement's spiritual profile in its early years. It was the practice in Kovno and Slobodka to spend the twilight hour when Sabbath was drawing to a close in an atmosphere suffused with sadness and grief, an atmosphere in which man loses his spiritual shield, his sense of power, confidence, and strength and becomes utterly sensitive and responsive, and there to engage in a monologue about death, the nihility of this world, its emptiness and ugliness. The halakhic men of Brisk and Volozhin sensed that this whole mood posed a profound contradiction to the Halakhah and would undermine its very foundations. Halakhic man fears nothing. For he swims in the sea of the Talmud, that life-giving sea to all the living. If a person has sinned, then the Halakhah of repentance will come to his aid. One must not waste time on spiritual self-appraisal, on probing introspections, and on the picking away at the

Focus on sin doesn't bring onto understanding of Torah.

"sense" of sin. Such a psychic analysis brings man neither to fear nor to love of God nor, most fundamental of all, to the knowledge and cognition of the Torah. The Torah cannot be acquired in a state of melancholia and depression. Man's entire psychic being must be committed to the regime of the cognition of Halakhah, and it is through such service that man can be saved from experiencing despair. The disjunctive emotions of fear and anxiety, if not rooted in Halakhah, will give rise to destructive consequences that will far outweigh any putative gains. R. Hayyim of Brisk's reply to R. Isaac Blaser, when the latter came to Volozhin in an attempt to persuade the heads of the yeshivah to introduce the study of Musar in their academy, is well known. R. Blaser, in support of his position, cited the statement of the sages: "A man should always incite the good impulse to fight against the evil impulse. . . . If he subdues it, well and good; if not, let him study the Torah. . . . If he subdues it, well and good; if not, let him . . . remind himself of the day of death" [Berakhot 5a]. Evidently, R. Blaser emphasized, the sages preferred the effectiveness of the remembrance of the day of death to the study of the Torah, for do we not have here stated that at times occupying oneself with Torah will not subdue the evil impulse while the remembrance of the day of death will vanquish it? R. Hayyim replied: If a person is sick we prescribe castor oil for him. However, it is certain that if a healthy person ingests castor oil he will become very sick. If that vile wretch [the evil impulse] meets you, and if you are sound in spirit and soul, if your consciousness and character are still whole and intact, occupy yourself with the Torah, drag him to the study house [see Sukkah 52b; Kiddushin 30b]. This is the most effective and tried remedy in man's ongoing battle with his evil impulse. However, if you are spiritually sick, if a fit of madness has seized hold of you, if some psychic anomaly has put forth its diseased tendrils in your inner world, then you must use more powerful drugs, those that are designed for the very ill—the remembrance of the day of death. We in Volozhin, thank God, are healthy in spirit and body, are whole in our Torah; there is no need here of castor oil. If the scholars of Kelm and Kovno feel compelled to drink bitter drugs—let them drink to their heart's content, but let them not invite others to dine with them.

In all truth and fairness it should be emphasized that when the Musar movement reached a state of maturity in the Yeshiva Knesset Israel under the directorship of R. Nathan Zvi Finkel and in the Mir Yeshiva under the spiritual guidance of R. Yeruham Levovitz, it assumed an entirely different form and approached the world perspective of the great halakhic men. The fear, the terror, the melancholy evaporated, and their place was taken by a powerful sense of the holiness and joy of life. The act of cognition in accordance with the Halakhah, new, original halakhic insights, spiritual creation, all replaced that exaggerated sensitivity and impressionability and that despairing perspective that had at first taken hold of the world of the Musar movement.

But, if halakhic man stays clear of melancholy and dread, he also recoils from any exaggerated spirit of joy, any sense of celebration lacking a healthy logical foundation, and any spiritual drunkenness. Halakhic man is characterized by an almost festive dignity (or, to use the term of William James, an attitude of solemnity.) [See *The Varieties of Religious Experience*, Lecture II, Circumscription of the Topic.] This stance prevents man from being attracted to any of the extremes of the emotional life and places a bar against his spirit, which tends at times to shatter all bounds of restraint and control. Whenever halakhic man rejoices, it is with the knowledge that this earthly life should not give rise to any exaggerated joy. Therefore, he does not exceed proper limits in times of happiness and jubilation. He fulfills the injunction of the Scriptures: "And rejoice with trembling" (Ps. 2:11). But in times of mourning and dejection, in moments of pain and grief as well, he is not crushed by his burden and is not given over to despair and black depression. His affective life is characterized by a fine equilibrium, a stoic tranquillity. It exemplifies the Aristotelian golden mean and the ideal of the well-balanced personality set forth by Maimonides; it is guided by the knowledge of inevitability and the means of triumphing over it provided by the rule of Halakhah. "He who does not mourn for his dead relative as prescribed by the sages is cruel; but he who grieves more than is customary is stupid."[89] This is the standard of halakhic man in the affective realm. Therefore, the great halakhists did not approve of wild dancing, unruly celebrations, and drunkenness (even for the sake of piety). It is related concerning the Gaon of Vilna how greatly he would rejoice on Simhat Torah during the *hakafot*. He would dance, clap, sing, and celebrate the occasion in a state of great rapture and enthusiasm. However, immediately afterward, upon the conclusion of the *hakafot*, he would revert back to his normal tranquil state. When the Gaon's brother died and the Gaon learned of it on the Sabbath [when mourning is forbidden], he did not display any emotion or signs of grief. After the Sabbath, when he concluded the *havdalah* he burst into tears. The beloved daughter of R. Elijah Pruzna [Feinstein] took sick about a month before she was to be married and after a few days was rapidly sinking. R. Elijah's son entered into the room where R. Elijah, wrapped in *tallit* and *tefillin*, was praying with the congregation, to tell him that his daughter was in her death throes. R. Elijah went into his daughter's room and asked the doctor how much longer it would be until the end. When he received the doctor's reply, R. Elijah returned to his room, removed his Rashi's *tefillin*, and quickly put on the *tefillin* prescribed by Rabbenu Tam, for immediately upon his daughter's death he would be an *onen*, a mourner whose dead relative has not as yet been buried, and as such would be subject to the law that an *onen* is exempt from all the commandments. After he removed his second pair of *tefillin*, wrapped them up, and put them away, he entered his dying daughter's room, in order to be present at the moment his most beloved daughter of all would return her soul back to its Maker. We have here great strength and presence of mind, the acceptance of the divine decree with love, the consciousness of the law and the judgment,[90] the might and power of the Halakhah, and faith, strong like flint.

XIII

individuality

OBVIOUSLY all these features contribute to the development of halakhic man's individuality. His character takes on its own particular hue, his autonomy asserts itself more and more, and his entire inner nature is determined by unique individual traits indicative of an ideal, noble personality. The will of *homo religiosus* gradually wanes to nothingness, and his selfhood is inexorably extinguished inasmuch as he desires to immerse himself in the totality of existence and to unite with infinity. Halakhic man, however, protects his own selfhood, his particularity, his soul's private domain. The "I," the self, is also part of that concrete reality which Halakhah purified and hallowed. In general, wherever the moral law reigns supreme, the sense of individuality becomes deeper and stronger. We have already explained above that *homo religiosus* oscillates between two opposing poles—the nullification of his existence on the one hand, and a feeling of self-exaltation reaching transcendental levels on the other. However, even when he makes a supreme effort to scale the transcendental heights, the effort is not motivated by a desire to perfect his individuality. The opposite is true. What *homo religiosus* wants is *unio mystica*, attachment to infinity and complete immersion and dissolution in the supernal realm.

In contrast to *homo religiosus*, halakhic man forges for himself a concrete, this-worldly personality. The maxim of Kant—that the moral law gives man the strength to stand before the overpowering cosmic drama without losing his own selfhood—

is well known. The a priori law molds man's permanent character and imprints its stamp upon his physiognomy. The countenance of the rabbinic scholar testifies to a strength of mind and a spiritual stature that sheds its brilliant light near and far. His whole being is imbued with the dignity of uniqueness and individuality, and displays a distinct streak of aristocracy. He is not a receptive type like *homo religiosus,* who stands and waits for the revelation of the truth and inspiration by the spirit. He does not search out transcendental, ecstatic paroxysms, frenzied experiences that whisper intimations of another world into his ears. He does not require any miracles or wonders in order to understand the Torah. He approaches the world of Halakhah with his mind and intellect, just as cognitive man approaches the natural realm. And since he relies upon his intellect, he places his trust in it and does not suppress any of his psychic faculties in order to merge into some supernal existence. His own personal understanding can resolve the most difficult and complex problems. He pays no heed to any murmurings of intuition or other types of mysterious presentiments. Halakhic man is a spontaneous, creative type. He is not particularly submissive and retiring, and is not meek when it is a matter of maintaining his own views. Neither modesty nor humility characterizes the image of halakhic man. On the contrary, his most characteristic feature is strength of mind. He does battle for every jot and tittle of the Halakhah, not only motivated by a deep piety but also by a passionate love of the truth. He recognizes no authority other than the authority of the intellect (obviously, in accordance with the principles of tradition). He hates intellectual compromises or fence straddling, intellectual flabbiness, and any type of wavering in matters of law and judgment.

This autonomy of the intellect at times reaches heights unimaginable in any other religion. The Talmud in Bava Metzia [86a] relates that there was a dispute between the Holy One, blessed be He, and the heavenly academy regarding a case where there is a doubt as to whether the bright spot [of a leper] preceded the white hair or the white hair preceded the bright spot. The Holy One, blessed be He, ruled: He is clean, while the heavenly academy ruled: He is unclean. And who was the arbiter? Rabbah bar Nahmani. Flesh and blood, mortal man decides between the Holy One, blessed be He, and the heavenly academy. When there was a dispute between R. Eliezer and the sages regarding the purity of the oven of Aknai, a heavenly voice declared: "Why do you disagree with R. Eliezer, seeing that in all matters the Halakhah is in accordance with his ruling?" R. Joshua arose and said: "'It is not in heaven' (Deut. 30:12). . . . For the Torah has already been given from Mount Sinai and we pay no attention to a heavenly voice." "And the Holy One, blessed be He, smiled in that hour and said: 'My children have defeated Me, My children have defeated Me.'"[91] More, if a prophet asserts "with reference to any law of the Torah, that the Lord has revealed to him that the law is thus or that the law is in accordance with so and so, he is a false prophet and is to be strangled even if he performed a sign, for he has come to contradict the Torah, which has stated 'It is not in heaven'."[92] The prophet, the transcendental man par excellence, has no right to encroach upon the domain of the sages, who decide the law on the basis on their intellect and knowledge. Halakhic man is a mighty ruler in the kingdom of spirit and intellect. Nothing can lead him astray; everything is subject to him, everything is under his sway and heeds his command. Even the Holy One, blessed be He, has, as it were, handed over His imprimatur, His official seal in Torah matters, to man; it is as if the Creator of the world Himself abides by man's decision and instruction. "R. Judah said: When the ministering angels gather together before God and ask Him: 'When is the New Year? When is the Day of Atonement?' God replies: 'Are you asking Me? Rather, I and you will go to the earthly court [to ask of it].' From whence can we derive this? It is written: 'For what great nation is there, that hath God [Elo-

him: plural form] so nigh unto them?' (Deut. 4:7). The verse does not state 'For what great nation is . . . so nigh unto Him?' but rather *Elohim*—i.e., God and His heavenly court are nigh [i.e., draw nigh] unto them. R. Judah said: [It is written: 'These are the festivals of the Lord, which ye shall proclaim' (Lev. 23:37)]. God said: Before Israel became My people, the festivals were 'the festivals of the Lord.' But henceforth the festivals are those 'which ye shall proclaim.'"[93] "'This month shall be unto you' (Exod. 12:2), to what may the matter be compared? To a king who had treasure-houses filled with gold, silver, and other precious stones and had an only son. As long as his son was still a minor, his father would watch over everything. When the son grew up and came of age, his father told him: As long as you were a minor, I would watch over everything. Now that you have come of age, I am turning over everything to you. Thus God would watch over everything. . . . When Israel came of age, He handed over everything to them."[94] The Holy One, blessed be He, has, as it were, stripped Himself of His ornaments—i.e., His dominion—and has handed it over to Israel, to the earthly court. The earthly court decrees, and the Holy One, blessed be He, complies. If the earthly court rules in matters of law and judgment, the Halakhah is always in accordance with its decision, even if the heavenly court should disagree. Halakhic man reigns over all and is esteemed by all. No other cognitive discipline has woven crowns for its heroes to the extent that the Halakhah has done. In no other field of knowledge has man been adorned with the crown of absolute royalty as in the realm of Torah. The glorification of man reaches here the peak of splendor.

Halakhic man received the Torah from Sinai not as a simple recipient but as a creator of worlds, as a partner with the Almighty in the act of creation. The power of creative interpretation (*ḥiddush*) is the very foundation of the received tradition. When Moses ascended on high, he found the Holy One, blessed be He, sitting there tying crowns to the letters in order that future generations should, by virtue of their powers of creative interpretation, discover heaps upon heaps of law contained in every tittle [see Menaḥot 29b]. All new, creative insights that a bright student will glean are an integral part of the Oral Law [see P. T. Peah 2:6; Lev. Rabbah 22:1]. "Only man is capable of creative interpretation (ḥiddush), something which is beyond the power of angels, for since the Holy One, blessed be He, created them in a state of perfection, they need not and, therefore, cannot develop and progress. But this is not the case with man, for he progresses and his intellect gains ever-increasing strength. Thus the sages have added fences and guards [around the law] which would not be possible had the Torah been given to the angels. For in that case it would remain forever unchanged, without addition or diminution."[95] The essence of the Torah is intellectual creativity. R. Hayyim Volozhin devoted the first chapter of his work *Nefesh ha-ḥayyim* to an explanation of the verse "And God created man in His own image, in the image of God created He him" (Gen. 1:27). The gist of his world perspective, to which he gives expression in his explanation, is that it is man who gives life to and constructs the worlds that are above him. The whole of transcendental existence is subjugated to him and under his sway. He creates supernal, exalted worlds and destroys them. "Know that which is higher *mimkha* ['than you' or 'from you']" [Avot 2:1]. All reality higher than our lowly world is from you; it exists by virtue of man's creative power. Know that [that] which is higher is from you![96]

XIV

IS halakhic man devoid of the splendor of that raging and tempestuous sacred, religious experience that so typifies the ecstatic *homo religiosus*? Can he attain such peaks of enthusiasm that he will cry out in rapture: "How manifold are

Thy works, O Lord! In wisdom hast Thou made them all" (Ps. 104:24). Is it possible for halakhic man to achieve such emotional exaltation that all his thoughts and senses ache and pine for the living God?

Halakhic man is worthy and fit to devote himself to a majestic religious experience in all its uniqueness, with all its delicate shades and hues. However, for him such a powerful, exalted experience only follows upon cognition, only occurs after he has acquired knowledge of the a priori, ideal Halakhah and its reflected image in the real world. But since this experience occurs after rigorous criticism and profound penetrating reflection, it is that much more intensive. To what may the matter be compared? To the physicist who concerns himself with mathematical formulae, the laws of mechanics, the laws of electromagnetic phenomena, optics, etc., etc. He joins together "precept to precept . . . line to line" (Isa. 28:10, 13), number to number; he engages in complex and difficult calculations, involving the manipulating of ideal, mathematical quantities that, at first glance, are wholly lacking in the music of the living world and the beauty of the resplendent cosmos. It would seem as if there exists no relationship between these quantities and reality. Yet these ideal numbers that cannot be grasped by one's senses, these numbers that only are meaningful from within the system itself, only meaningful as part of abstract mathematical functions, symbolize the image of existence. Is not the physicist swept to heights of rapture in the act of cognizing the world? Did not Newton delight in the beauty of the world when he discovered the law of gravity or, simultaneously, with Leibnitz,[97] the differential and integral calculus? "Precept to precept, precept to precept, line to line, line to line; here a little, there a little" (Isa. 28:10, 13), number to number, quantity to quantity, function to function, one physical law to another physical law, and as a result of scientific man's creativity there arises an ordered, illumined, determined world, imprinted with the stamp of the creative intellect, of pure reason and clear cognition. From the midst of the order and lawfulness we hear a new song, the song of the creature to the Creator, the song of the cosmos to its Maker. Not only the qualitative light, perceptible to the senses, with its wealth of hues and shades, its whirl of colors, sings to the Holy One, blessed be He; so do the quantitative light waves as well, the fruit of cognitive man's knowledge. Not only the qualitative world bursts forth in song, but so does the quantitative world. From the very midst of the laws there arises a cosmos more splendid and beautiful than all the works of Leonardo da Vinci and Michelangelo. Perhaps these experiences of cognitive man are lacking in the emotional dynamic and turbulent passion of aesthetic man; perhaps these experiences are devoid of flashy and externally impressive bursts of ecstasy or stychic enthusiasm. However, they are possessed of a profound depth and a clear penetrating vision. They do not flourish and then wither away like experiences that are only based upon a vague, obscure moment of psychic upheaval. Such an experience is not some fleeting, unstable phenomenon that ebbs and flows, but is fixed and determined, possessed of a clear and firmly established countenance of its own. So is it also with halakhic man. His religious experience is mature and ripe when he cognizes the world through the prism of the Halakhah. Halakhic man will not dance in the streets on the Passover night, nor will he shout out his prayers on the Days of Awe; but this is not to say that he is not inspired and excited by sacred time or that he is lacking in a powerful religious experience. The halakhic man who cognizes sacred time, who realizes, for example, that the Day of Atonement carries with it absolution or who knows the laws of Passover, and specifically the laws of Passover night, that night which imposes upon him additional commandments—song, *matzah, maror,* the recitation of the Exodus, etc., etc.—is not devoid of a mighty and forceful religious experience. This experience is arrived at, to be sure, through contemplative reflection, but it is in no way inferior to the experience of the universal *homo religiosus.* This experience is modest, retiring, very delicate, but strong as flint. In general we can set it down as a firmly established rule that any religious experience which is based upon all-encompassing cognition and profound understanding is exceptionally consistent, intensive, and long lasting. At times we may tend to look askance upon that religiosity which follows cognition, for does it not seem somewhat pallid, overly refined, indeed fastidious? However these characteristics are in truth a highly auspicious sign. Halakhic man, also, after he has perfected his ideal world with laws, statutes, judgments, decrees, stringencies, legal details, and particulars, does not remain fastened to the realm of the particular but betakes himself to the realm of the universal, to the idea of wholeness. Halakhic man also, whose hands are soiled with the gritty realia of practical Halakhah, with an endless stream of laws, an innumerable amount of halakhot, constructs a world perspective that embraces the whole vast range of existence. "He who walks by the way and studies and breaks off his study and says, 'How beautiful is this tree, how beautiful is this fallow,' Scripture counts it to him as if he committed a mortal sin" [Avot 3:8]. Cognition should precede rapture; he who reaches a peak of enthusiasm prior to his having cognized, prior to his having completed his study, it is as if he has committed a mortal sin. The tones of *amor Dei intellectualis,* the intellectual love of God, are reverberating here. And, indeed, how beautiful is the echo of these tones, if the God for whom man longs is the living God and not an impersonal, infinite substance, imprinted with the stamp of necessity.

The approach to God is also made possible by the Halakhah. Primarily, halakhic man cognizes God via His Torah, via the truth of halakhic cognition. There is truth in the Halakhah, there is a halakhic epistemology, there is a halahkic thinking "the measure thereof is longer than the earth" (Job 11:9). There is a Torah wisdom "that is broader than the sea" (ibid). And all of these are rooted in the will of the Holy One, blessed be He, the revealer of the Law. This approach is not an ethical-practical approach, like that of Kant and Hermann Cohen, but a theoretical-normative one. It is via the ideal world, in which creation and the norm blend together, that man approaches God. We require neither miracles nor wonder to prove the existence of God, for the Halakhah itself bears witness to its Creator. To be sure, we can also find in the Halakhah a practical approach to God, an approach to God through the performance of the commandments in a concrete fashion. But this approach only follows in the wake of the first approach. The primary approach to God is the ideal-normative-theoretical relationship that prevails between God and halakhic man.

Halakhic man is not a man of words. Thought and speech, the meditation of the heart and the articulated word, logos qua thought and logos qua speech, constitute an old problem in philosophy. Logic and grammar, the logical judgment and the grammatical sentence, represent an ancient crux over which much ink has been spilt and many pens have been broken. Cognitive man prefers thought to speech, logic to statements. He is neither a rhetorician nor a master of the fine phrase. Language for him is not an end in itself, but only a means for the formulation of thought. When cognitive man uses language, he takes particular care not to multiply needlessly words or phrases. Too much is as bad as too little. If anything, his language is overflowing with ideas. Every sentence expresses a thought, every phrase a concept. If an idea can be expressed in three words, he will not use four. Additional words do not serve to clarify or elucidate a particular matter but only to obscure it. Cognitive man takes particular care that there should exist a precise correlation between each word and the kernel of cognitive content contained within it. He does not fling about terms and phrases as a substitute for thought and reflection. The thought matures and ripens, and only then can the words come. The thinking logos precedes the speaking logos. Halakhic man, in this respect, resembles cognitive man. Among halakhists who typify this characteristic are Rashi, Maimonides, the Gaon of Vilna, and R. Hayyim of Brisk, all of whom strictly limited themselves in their use of words but soared to the furthest expanses on the wings of thought. Every jot and tittle of Rashi's commentary on the Talmud and Maimonides's *Mishneh Torah* allude to heaps and heaps of halakhot. The word *ve-ayen*—i.e., "cf." in the Gaon's commentary on the *Shulkhan Arukh*—contains treasure-houses of thought. Each and every sentence in the writings of R. Hayyim constitutes a flowing spring of creative insight and cognition. When ecstasy seizes hold of *homo religiosus,* he bursts forth in song and psalm and is very casual with the phrases and linguistic forms he uses. Halakhic man, on the contrary, is very sparing in his recitation of the piyyutim, not, heaven forbid, on account of philosophical qualms,[98] but because he serves his Maker with pure halakhic thought, precise cognition, and clear logic. He does not waste his time reciting songs and hymns. The cognition of the Torah—this is the holiest and most exalted type of service. He serves the Creator by uncovering the truth in the Halakhah, by solving difficulties and resolving problems. Once my father entered the synagogue on Rosh Ha-Shanah, late in the afternoon, after the regular prayers were over, and found me reciting Psalms with the congregation. He took away my Psalm book and handed me a copy of the tractate Rosh Ha-Shanah. "If you wish to serve the Creator at this moment, better study the laws pertaining to the festival." While the congregation would recite piyyutim on the Days of Awe, R. Hayyim would study Torah. On Rosh Ha-Shanah he would study the laws of *shofar,* on the Day of Atonement the laws pertaining to the sacrificial order of the day. God Himself sits and studies the Torah and "God only has in His world the four cubits of the Halakhah"[99] [Berakhot 8a]. The study of the Torah is not a means to another end, but is the end point of all desires. It is the most fundamental principle of all.

"The whole notion of [Torah] *lishmah* ['for its own sake' or 'for the sake of the (Divine) Name'] primarily refers to [study-ing] for the sake of the love of the Torah—i.e., that one should exert oneself to determine the root principle [of the law]. But a person may think that *lishmah* means [for the sake of] cleaving [to God], and, therefore, according to this opinion it would be preferable for one to occupy oneself with songs and hymns and in particular with the Psalms of [David,] the sweet singer of Israel, that arouse in one love for God and a sense of His closeness, and this is sufficient for him and in this man-ner he will attain a pleasant life. But such is not the case. For the Midrash [on Psalms 1:8] states that King David re-quested that God should account one who would recite the Psalms as being on the same level as one who studies the laws of leprosy and tents. This clearly implies that the study of these laws is of more value than the recitation of Psalms. And there is no indication [in the Midrash] that God granted him his request. This is so because the primary purpose of study is not to study simply for the sake of cleaving to God, but to com-prehend, through the Torah, the commandments and laws, and to know each and every matter clearly, both its general principles and its particulars. . . . Thus one should study these matters—i.e., these laws—for the sake of the matters them-selves . . .—so that one will comprehend these matters and deepen one's understanding and analytic skill and not study simply for the sake of cleaving [to God], as many have errone-ously thought. Rather, one must delve profoundly and inquire into the very concrete materiality of these laws. For example, when one studies civil law, one must at times closely analyze the issue of *miggo* [i.e., the principle that a party's plea is to be credited if a more convenient or a more advantageous plea is available to him]. Now *miggo* raises the question of [the psy-chology of] liars—i.e., we ask ourselves if a particular party were a liar, what type of plea might he put forward. . . . Thus even though at the time of study a person does not have the fear of God in mind, nevertheless the study itself is for the sake of the unification of the Holy One, blessed be He. Therefore, when a person exerts himself to understand a halakhic matter clearly, then it is certain that the *Shekhinah,* the Divine Presence, rests upon him at the very moment he is studying. As the sages have stated: 'God only has in His world the four cubits of the Halakhah.'"[100]

The above is the declaration of R. Hayyim Volozhin, the outstanding student of the Gaon of Vilna and the founder of the Yeshivah of Volozhin; and it would appear to me that it needs no comment.

XV

HALAKHIC man does not quiver before any man; he does not seek out compliments, nor does he require public approval. If he sees that there are fewer and fewer men of distinguished spiritual rank about, then he wraps himself in his mantle and hies away to the four cubits of Halakhah. He knows that the truth is a lamp unto his feet and the Halakhah a light unto his path. His whole being loathes idlers, wastrels, and loafers. Piety that is not based upon knowledge of the Torah is of no consequence in his view. There can be no fear of God without knowledge and no service of God without the cognition of halakhic truth. "A crude man fears not sin, nor is a man ignorant of Torah pious" [Avot 2:5]. The old saying of Socrates, that virtue is knowledge, is strikingly similar to the stance of halakhic man.

And this halakhic truth is one complete and ultimate truth, which halakhic man is not ready to sacrifice even for the sake of some exalted goal. He does not understand the ins and outs of politics, nor is he cunning (I am not speaking of wisdom) in worldly matters. He will not overlook a single jot or tittle of the Halakhah, even to realize some lofty desire. We have here manifested not the religious zeal of the universal *homo religiosus* but a type of zeal specific to the halakhist—the zeal for the truth, granted him by the Almighty. Thus, halakhic man will not be overly lenient; but, at the same time, he will not be overly strict. The truth will call to account those who dishonor it, be they extreme rigorists or extreme permissivists.

Once R. Hayyim of Brisk was attending a conference of outstanding Torah scholars in St. Petersburg. The item on the agenda was the question of uncircumcised infants—should their names be entered in the official register of the Jewish community. All of the rabbis declared: "It is certainly forbidden to register them, for they are not circumcised." (Through this tactic they hoped to compel the assimilationists to circumcise their sons.) R. Hayyim arose and said: "My masters, please show me the halakhah which states that one who is not circumcised is not a member of the Jewish people. I am aware that a person who is not circumcised may not partake of the sacrifices or the heave offering, but I am unaware that he is devoid of the holiness belonging to the Jewish people. To be sure, if he comes of age and does not circumcise himself he is liable to excision.[101] However, he who eats blood and he who violates the Sabbath are also liable to excision. Why then do you treat the uncircumcised infant so stringently and the Sabbath violator so leniently? On the contrary, this infant has not as yet sinned at all, except that his father has not fulfilled his obligation." From a political and practical perspective, and as an emergency measure, no doubt the majority was correct. However, on the basis of the pure Halakhah, R. Hayyim was correct. And he would not sacrifice this halakhic truth even for the sake of realizing the noblest of ideas.

Halakhic man implements the Torah without any compromises or concessions, for precisely such implementation, such actualization is his ultimate desire, his fondest dream. When a person actualizes the ideal Halakhah in the very midst of the real world, he approaches the level of that godly man, the prophet—the creator of worlds. Therefore, the ideals of righteousness, which the Torah first introduced into the world, are implemented, are actualized and concretized, by halakhists in all their purity and resplendent brilliance. Halakhic man cannot be cowed by anyone. He knows no fear of flesh and blood. For is he not a creator of worlds, a partner of the Almighty in the act of creation? And precisely because he is free from fear of flesh and blood, he neither betrays his own mission nor profanes his holy task. He takes up his stand in the midst of the concrete world, his feet planted firmly on the ground of reality, and he looks about and sees, listens and hears, and publicly protests against the oppression of the helpless, the defrauding of the poor, the plight of the orphan. The rich are deemed as naught in his view. He is the father of orphans, the judge of widows. My uncle, R. Meir Berlin [Bar-Ilan], told me that once R. Hayyim of Brisk was asked what the function of a rabbi is. R. Hayyim replied: "To redress the grievances of those who are abandoned and alone, to protect the dignity of the poor, and to save the oppressed from the hands of his oppressor." Neither ritual decisions nor political leadership constitutes the main task of halakhic man. Far from it. The actualization of the ideals of justice and righteousness is the pillar of fire which halakhic man follows, when he, as a rabbi and teacher in Israel, serves his community. More, through the implementation of the principles of righteousness, man fulfills the task of creation imposed upon him: the perfection of the world under the dominion of Halakhah and the renewal of the face of creation. No religious cult is of any worth if the laws and principles of righteousness are violated and trampled upon by the foot of pride. "A precept that is fulfilled through a transgression," attaining religious ends through unjust means, is of absolutely no value. "For I the Lord love justice, I hate robbery with a burnt offering" (Isa. 61:8). Iniquity prevents man's prayer from being accepted on high. The anguish of the poor, the despair of the helpless and humiliated outweigh many many commandments. "He who shames his fellow man in public has no share in the world to come" [Avot 3:15; Bava Metzia 59a]. If a person sinned against his fellow man, repentance and the Day of Atonement cannot grant him atonement until he has appeased his fellow [Yoma 8:5; Maimonides, *Laws of Repentance* 7:9].

That dualism, so prevalent in other religions, which distinguishes between the man who stands before the Lord in an atmosphere suffused with heavenly solemnity and the man driving a hard bargain with his fellow in the marketplace, is totally foreign to the Halakhah. We have already emphasized earlier that Judaism does not direct its glance upward but downward. The Halakhah does not aspire to a heavenly transcendence, nor does it seek to soar upon the wings of some abstract, mysterious spirituality. It fixes its gaze upon concrete, empirical reality and does not allow its attention to be diverted from it. Halakhic man does not compartmentalize reality—this is the domain of eternal life and this the domain of temporal life. On the contrary, he brings down eternity into the midst of time. He does not enter into a hidden, pure, transcendent realm even in his intimate prayer-colloquy with his Creator. Even when halakhic man enters the synagogue or study house, he does not leave his this-worldly life behind. His prayer is replete with requests regarding bodily needs: healing, prosperity, political freedom, a good and peaceful life, and such. The strange, disturbing dualism that blossoms forth in other religions is grounded in the fragmentation of life into many different sectors. The universal *homo religiosus* not infrequently sets up markers and draws sweeping demarcation lines—till here is the divine-heavenly-transcendental realm and from this point on the realm of earthly, bodily life. *Homo religiosus,* praying in his house of worship, prostrated on the cold stone floor, repeating over and over the old litany *non mea voluntas sed tua fiat*—not my will be done, only Thine—is not at that moment a this-worldly man, possessor of riches and chattels, estates and factories, who drives his impoverished workers ruthlessly, and whose hands are often stained with the blood of the outcast and the ill-gotten gain wrung from the hands of the unfortunate. For him the world of prayer and the world of reality have nothing to do with each other. He enters his sanctuary humble and contrite, in a mood of submission and humility. In this religious atmosphere filled with the thick clouds of incense and the echoes of the hymns of angels and seraphim, he divests himself of his arrogance, of his rigid, unbending character, and becomes the very model of meekness, self-effacing and bowed down. And he leaves the same way he entered, humble and submissive [cf. Sanhedrin 88b]. However, no sooner does he step outside into the noisy, clamorous street than he reverts back to his original persona, to his previous haughty and conceited self-centeredness. The heavenly kingdom does not come into the slightest contact with the earthly kingdom. This mode of behavior cannot even be considered a form of flattery or religious obsequiousness. It is rather a manifestation of a strange, obscure, psychic dualism whose nature cannot be determined. The man in the sanctuary and the man in the marketplace are two separate and distinct personalities who have absolutely nothing in common with one another. How many noblemen bowed down before the cross in a spirit of abject submission and self-denial, confessed their sins with scalding tears and bitter cries and in the very same breath, as soon as they left the dim precincts of the cathedral, ordered that innocent people be cruelly slain. We have here a manifestation of a deep fissure in one's psychic identity. The Halakhah, however, rejects such a personality split, such a spiritual schizophrenia. It does not differentiate between the man who stands in his house of worship, engaged in ritual activities, and the mortal who must wage the arduous battle of life. The Halakhah declares that man stands before God not only in the synagogue but also in the public domain, in his house, while on a journey, while lying down and rising up. "And thou shalt talk of them when thou sittest in thy house, and when thou walkest by the way, and when thou liest down and when thou risest up" (Deut. 6:7).

The primary difference between halakhic man and *homo religiosus* is that while the latter prefers the spirit to the body, the soul to its mortal frame, as the main actor in the religious drama, the former, as has been stated above, wishes to sanctify the physical-biological concrete man as the hero and protagonist of religious life. Therefore, the whole notion of ritual assumes a special form in Judaism. The standard notion of ritual prevalent among religious men—i.e., ritual as a nonrational religious act whose whole purpose is to lift man up from concrete reality to celestial realms—is totally foreign to Judaism. According to the outlook of Halakhah, the service of God (with the exception of the study of the Torah) can be carried out only through the implementation, the actualization of its principles in the real world. The ideal of righteousness is the guiding light of this world-view. Halakhic man's most fervent desire is the perfection of the world under the dominion of righteousness and loving-kindness—the realization of the a priori, ideal creation, whose name is Torah (or Halakhah), in the realm of concrete life. The Halakhah is not hermetically enclosed within the confines of cult sanctuaries but penetrates into every nook and cranny of life. The marketplace, the street, the factory, the house, the meeting place, the banquet hall, all constitute the backdrop for the religious life. The synagogue does not occupy a central place in Judaism.

When liberal Judaism expelled the *Shekhinah,* the Divine Presence, from the broad arena of Jewish life, it set aside a special place for it in the temple. As a result, according to the liberal Jewish outlook, the temple stands at the heart of religion. The Halakhah, the Judaism that is faithful to itself, however, which brings the Divine Presence into the midst of empirical reality, does not center about the synagogue or study house. These are minor sanctuaries. The true sanctuary is the sphere of our daily, mundane activities, for it is there that the realization of the Halakhah takes place. The great Torah giants, the halakhic men, par excellence, were indeed champions of truth and justice. They glowed with a resplendent ethical beauty. Space does not permit me even to begin to speak, for example, about R. Hayyim's unrelenting efforts to realize the ideals of righteousness and equity. Let me merely cite one incident wherewith to conclude this section. Once two Jews died in Brisk on the same day. In the morning a poor shoemaker who had lived out his life in obscurity died, while about noontime a wealthy, prominent member of the community passed away. According to the Halakhah, in such a case the one who dies first must be buried first. However the members of the burial society, who had received a handsome sum from the heirs of the rich man, decided to attend to him first, despite the fact that he had died later, for who was there to plead the cause of the poor man? When R. Hayyim was informed about the incident, he sent a messenger of the court to warn the members of the burial society to desist from their disgraceful behavior. The members of the burial society, however, refused to heed the directive of R. Hayyim and began to make the arrangements for the burial of the rich man. R. Hayyim then arose, took his walking stick, trudged over to the house of the deceased, and chased all the attendants outside. R. Hayyim prevailed—the poor man was buried before the rich man. R. Hayyim's enemies multiplied and increased.

Thus have true halakhic men always acted, for their study and their deeds have blended together beautifully, truly beautifully.

PART TWO

HALAKHIC MAN

His Creative Capacity

H ALAKHIC man is a man who longs to create, to bring into being something new, something original. The study of Torah, by definition, means gleaning new, creative insights from the Torah (*ḥiddushei Torah*). "The Holy One, blessed be He, rejoices in the dialectics of Torah" [a popular folk saying]. Read not here 'dialectics' (*pilpul*) but 'creative interpretation' (*ḥiddush*). This notion of *ḥiddush*, of creative interpretation, is not limited solely to the theoretical domain but extends as well into the practical domain, into the real world. The most fervent desire of halakhic man is to behold the replenishment of the deficiency in creation, when the real world will conform to the ideal world and the most exalted and glorious of creations, the ideal Halakhah, will be actualized in its midst. The dream of creation is the central idea in the halakhic consciousness—the idea of the importance of man as a partner of the Almighty in the act of creation, man as creator of worlds. This longing for creation and the renewal of the cosmos is embodied in all of Judaism's goals. And if at times we raise the question of the ultimate aim of Judaism, of the telos of the Halakhah in all its multifold aspects and manifestations, we must not disregard the fact that this wondrous spectacle of the creation of worlds is the Jewish people's eschatological vision, the realization of all its hopes.

The Halakhah sees the entire Torah as consisting of basic laws and halakhic principles. Even the Scriptural narratives serve the purpose of determining everlasting law. "The mere conversations of the servants of the fathers are more important than the laws [Torah] of the sons. The chapter dealing with Eliezer covers two or three columns, and [his conversation] is not only recorded but repeated. Whereas [the uncleanliness of] a reptile is a basic principle of Torah law [*gufei Torah*], yet it is only from an extending particle in the Scriptures that we know that its blood defiles as flesh" (Gen. Rabbah 60:11). Our Torah does not contain even one superfluous word or phrase. Each letter alludes to basic principles of Torah law, each word to "well-fastened," authoritative, everlasting halakhot. From beginning to end it is replete with statutes and judgments, commandments and laws. The mystics discern in our Torah divine mysteries, esoteric teachings, the secrets of creation, and the *Merkabah* [the chariot of Ezekiel's prophecy];[102] the halakhic sages discern in it basic halakhot, practical principles, laws, directives, and statutes. "The deeds of the fathers are a sign for the sons" [cf. Nahmanides, *Commentary on the Torah*, Gen. 12:6]. And this sign—i.e., the vision of the future—constitutes a clear-cut halakhah. Halakhic man discerns in every divine pledge man's obligation to bring about its fulfillment, in every promise a specific norm, in every eschatological vision an everlasting commandment (the commandment to participate in the realization of the prophecy). The conversations of the servants, the trials of the fathers, the fate of the tribes, all teach the sons Torah and commandments. The conversations of the servants of the fathers are, in truth, the Torah of the sons. The only difference between the conversation of Eliezer and the Scriptural portion concerning the reptile is that the former extends over two or three columns while the latter is but a brief passage.

Therefore, if the Torah spoke at length about the creation of the world and related to us the story of the making of heaven and earth and all their host, it did so not in order to reveal cosmogonic secrets and metaphysical mysteries but rather in order to teach *practical* Halakhah. The Scriptural portion of the creation narrative is a legal portion, in which are to be found basic, everlasting halakhic principles, just like the portion of *Kedoshim* (Lev. 19) or *Mishpatim* (Exod. 21). If the Torah then chose to relate to man the tale of creation, we may clearly derive one law from this manner of procedure—viz., that man is obliged to engage in creation and the renewal of the cosmos.[103]

Not for naught is Judaism acquainted with a Book of Creation, the mastery of which enables one both to create and destroy worlds. "Raba said: If the righteous desired it, they could be creators of worlds, as it is written, 'But your iniquities have separated between you and your God' (Isa. 59:2). (Rashi explains: We may infer from this that if they would not have any iniquities, there would be no distinction [between man and God, in the matter of creation]). Raba created a man. . . . R. Hanina and R. Oshia spent every Sabbath eve in studying the Book of Creation and created a third-grown calf" (Sanhedrin 65b).

The peak of religious ethical perfection to which Judaism aspires is man as creator.

When God created the world, He provided an opportunity for the work of His hands—man—to participate in His creation. The Creator, as it were, impaired reality in order that mortal man could repair its flaws and perfect it. God gave the Book of Creation—that repository of the mysteries of creation—to man, not simply for the sake of theoretical study but in order that man might continue the act of creation. "As soon as Abraham had understood, fashioned, engraved, attached and created, inquired and clearly grasped [the secret of creation], the Lord of the universe revealed Himself to him, called him His friend, and made a covenant with him between the ten fingers of his hand. . . ."[104] Man's task is to "fashion, engrave, attach, and create," and transform the emptiness in being into a perfect and holy existence, bearing the imprint of the divine name.

"The earth was chaos and void, and darkness was upon the

face of the deep. . . . And God said: 'Let there be light'; and there was light. . . . God divided the light from the darkness. God called the light Day and the darkness He called Night. . . . Let there be a firmament in the midst of the waters, and let it divide the waters from the waters. . . . Let the waters under the heavens be gathered together unto one place, and let the dry land appear. . . . God called the dry land Earth, and the gathering of the waters He called Seas, etc." (Gen. 1:2–10).

When God engraved and carved out the world, he did not entirely eradicate the chaos and the void, the deep, the darkness, from the domain of His creation. Rather, he separated the complete, perfect existence from the forces of negation, confusion, and turmoil and set up cosmic boundaries, eternal laws to keep them apart. Now Judaism affirms the principle of creation out of absolute nothingness. Therefore, the chaos and the void, the deep, the darkness, and relative nothingness must all have been fashioned by the Almighty before the creation of the orderly, majestic, beautiful world. "A philosopher once said to Rabban Gamliel: Your God is a great artist, but He found good materials which helped Him: chaos and the void, the deep, the wind [*ruah*], water and darkness. He replied: Let the bones of that person [who so averred] be blasted! For the Scripture affirms that all these things were created. With regard to chaos and the void it is written: 'I [God] make peace, and create evil' (Isa. 45:7); with regard to darkness it is written: 'I form the light and create darkness' (Isa. 45:7); with regard to the wind [*ruah*] it is written: 'He formeth the mountains, and createth the wind [*ruah*]' (Amos 4:13); with regard to the deep it is written: 'Out of nothing I carved out the deep' (Prov. 8:24)" [Gen. Rabbah 1:12]. All of these "primordial" materials were created in order that they subsist and be located in the world itself. Not for naught did He create them. He created them in order that they may dwell within the cosmos!

However, the forces of relative nothingness at times exceed their bounds. They wish to burst forth out of the chains of obedience that the Almighty imposed upon them and seek to plunge the earth back into chaos and the void. It is only the law that holds them back and bars the path before them. Now the Hebrew term for law, *ḥok,* comes from the root *ḥ-k-k* (which means "to carve, engrave"). Thus the law carves out a boundary, sets up markers, establishes special domains, all for the purpose of separating existence from "nothingness," the ordered cosmos from the void, and creation from the naught. "When He carved [*ḥok*] a circle [*ḥug*] upon the face of the deep" (Prov. 8:27)—*ḥok,* the carving, the engraving, the law=*ḥug,* the circle=an all-encompassing boundary.[105] The perfect and complete ontic being extends until this divinely carved-out boundary; beyond that border is the deep, chaos and the void, darkness, and the "nothingness," devoid of image and form.

However, this relative "nothingness" is plotting evil, the deep is devising iniquity, and the chaos and void lie in wait in the dark alleyways of reality and seek to undermine the absolute being, to profane the lustrous image of creation. "Thou didst cover it with the deep as with a vesture; the waters stood above the mountains. At Thy rebuke they fled, at the sound of Thy thunder they hastened away. . . . Thou didst set a bound which they should not pass over, that they might return to cover the earth" (Ps. 104:6–9). "When He assigned to the sea its limit, so that the waters might not transgress His command, when He carved out the foundations of the earth"(Prov. 8:29). The deep wishes to cast off the yoke of the law (*ḥok*), to pass beyond the boundary (*ḥug*) and limit that the Creator set up and carved out and inundate the world and the fullness thereof. However, at the rebuke of the Almighty, it flees in retreat. From the sound of His thunder it is driven back and hastens to its "lair"—the lair of nothingness. The sight of a tempestuous sea, of whirling, raging waves that beat upon the shore there to break, symbolizes to the Judaic consciousness the struggle of the chaos and void with creation, the quarrel of the deep with the principles of order and the battle of confusion with the law.

The mysterious power of the delineated law and the limiting boundary which the Almighty implanted in existence presented itself in all its awesomeness and majesty to King David, the sweet singer of Israel, as reflected in the natural phenomenon of the orderly ebb and flow of the sea (caused by the gravitational force of the sun and the moon and the rotation of the earth). The sea at high tide and the sea at low tide appeared in their whirl of colors as a symbolic elemental process, as a bewitching spectacle of an eternal clash of forces. It is as though the sea at high tide, rushing to meet the shore, desires to destroy the boundary and the law, as though the disorder of the primordial forces, of chaos and confusion, desires to cleave asunder the perfect and exquisitely chiseled creation and lay it waste. Only the mighty strength of the law of the Almighty bars the path before them [the waves] and shatters them. "Thou rulest the proud swelling of the sea; when the waves thereof arise, Thou dost shatter them" (Ps. 89:10).

"R. Johanan said: When David dug the pits, the deep arose and threatened to submerge the world. . . . David thereupon inscribed the ineffable name upon a sherd, cast it into the deep, and it subsided."[106] "When David began to dig the foundations of the Temple, he dug 15 cubits and did not reach the deep. Finally he found one potsherd and sought to lift it up. Said [the potsherd] unto him: You may not. Said [David] unto it: And why not? Said [the potsherd] unto David: Because it is I who am restraining the deep. Said [David] unto it: And for how long have you been here? Said [the potsherd] unto him: Since the Almighty proclaimed on Mount Sinai 'I am the Lord thy God' (Exod. 20:2). At that moment the earth trembled and began to sink and I was placed here to restrain the deep. David, nevertheless, did not listen to it. As soon as he lifted it, the waters of the deep arose and sought to inundate the world."[107] Thus the deep desires to burst out of the enclosures of the law and shatter the realms of orderly creation, the cosmic process, the regular course of the world, and plunge them all back into "nothingness," into desolation and ontic emptiness. However, it is held firm in the grip of the mighty law and its principles.[108]

All of kabbalistic literature is imbued with this idea. The "other side," the "husks," the "mighty deep," the "angels of destruction," the "offspring of chaos," etc., all symbolize the realm of emptiness and the void, the domain of "nothingness," devoid of any image or stature,[109] that does battle with the glorious existence enveloped by the luster of the image of the Divine Presence.

However, this view, which threads its way through the entire course of Jewish thought, is not just a mysterious theoretical notion but a practical principle, a fundamental ethico-halakhic postulate.

II

WHEN man, the crowning glory of the cosmos, approaches the world, he finds his task at hand—the task of creation. He must stand on guard over the pure, clear existence, repair the defects in the cosmos, and replenish the "privation" in being. Man, the creature, is commanded to become a partner with the Creator in the renewal of the cosmos; complete and ultimate creation—this is the deepest desire of the Jewish people.

The Scriptural text "And the heaven and the earth were finished, and all the host of them" (Gen. 2:1)—the Targum, the Aramaic translation of the Pentateuch, translates *va-yekhulu,* "were finished," as *ve-ishtakhlelu,* "were perfected"—is both a profound expression of the soul of the people and the most fervent desire of the man of God. This lofty, ontological idea illumines the path of the eternal people. When a Jew on the Sabbath eve recites [this passage as part of] the *kiddush,* the sanctification over the wine, he testifies not only to the existence of a Creator but also to man's obligation to become a partner with the Almighty in the continuation and perfection of His creation. Just as the Almighty constantly refined and improved the realm of existence during the six days of creation, so must man complete that creation and transform the domain of chaos and void into a perfect and beautiful reality.

When a Jew goes outside and beholds the pale moon casting its delicate strands of light into the empty reaches of the world, he recites a blessing. The natural, orderly, cosmic phenomenon precipitates in his religious consciousness both melancholy thoughts and bright hopes. He contemplates this spectacle of the lawful cycle of the waxing and waning of the moon and sees in it a symbol of defectiveness and renewal. Just as the moon is "defective" and then "renewed," so creation is "defective" and will be "renewed," "replenished." To be sure, God "with His word created the heavens. [He] gave them a fixed time so that they should not alter their appointed charges" [from the blessing over the new moon]. We are not speaking here about any mythological notions, heaven forbid, but about the cognition of the natural law governing the courses of the heavenly hosts based upon clear, precise astronomical knowledge. However, the law itself, the orderly movement itself, symbolizes a wondrous mystery. The very court which would make its astronomical calculations "in the same manner as the astronomers, who discern positions and motions of stars, engage in calculations,"[110] would go outside and recite a blessing over the new moon. The Jewish people see in the orderly and lawful motion of the moon in its orbit a process of defectiveness and renewal, the defectiveness of the creation and its renewal, its replenishment. They, therefore, whisper a strange silent prayer: "May it be Thy will . . . to replenish the defect of the moon so that there be in it no diminution. And let the light of the moon be like the light of the sun, like the light of creation, like it was before it was diminished. As it is said: 'And God made the two great lights' (Gen. 1:16)" [from the prayer following the blessing over the new moon]. The Jewish people, by means of this prayer, give allegorical expression to their hope for the perfection of creation and the repairing of the defects in the cosmos, to their hope for the realization of that great and awesome symbolic eschatological vision: "The light of the moon shall be as the light of the sun" (Isa. 30:26)[111]

Examining matters from this esoteric vantage point, the Jewish people see their own fate as bound up with the fate of existence as a whole, that existence which is impaired and cleft asunder by the forces of negation and "nothingness." Physical reality and spiritual-historical existence—both have suffered greatly on account of the dominion of the abyss, of chaos and the void, and their fates parallel one another. When the historical process of the Jewish people reaches its consummation and attains the heights of perfection, then (in an allegorical sense) the flaws of creation as a whole will also be repaired. "He bade the moon renew itself for those who were burdened from birth, who like her will be renewed and will extol their Creator on account of the name of His glorious kingdom" [from the blessing over the new moon].

Man is obliged to perfect what his Creator "impaired." "Resh Lakish said: Why is the new-moon goat offering different, in that [the phrase] 'a sin offering unto the Lord' (Num. 28:15) is used in connection with it [whereas ordinarily the phrase 'a sin offering' is used without the additional 'unto the Lord']? Because the Holy One, blessed be He, said: This goat shall be an atonement for My diminishing the moon [i.e., it is as if the sin offering is not 'unto the Lord' but 'on behalf of the Lord']."[112] The Jewish people bring a sacrifice to atone, as it were, for the Holy One, blessed be He, for not having completed the work of creation.[113] The Creator of the world diminished the image and stature of creation in order to leave something for man, the work of His hands, to do, in order to adorn man with the crown of creator and maker.[114]

The perfection of creation, according to the view of halakhic man, is expressed in the actualization of the ideal Halakhah in the real world. And once again we see revealed before us the divergent approaches of the Halakhah and mysticism. While mysticism repairs the flaws of creation by "raising it on high," by returning it back to the source of pure, clear existence, the Halakhah fills the "deficiency" by drawing the *Shekhinah*, the Divine Presence, downward into the lowly world, by "contracting" transcendence within our flawed world.

A new aspect of the idea of holiness arises here. We have already emphasized, that while the universal *homo religiosus* understands the concept of holiness as a rebellion against this world, as a daring attempt to scale the very heights of transcendence, Judaism explains the concept of holiness from the perspective of the secret of "contraction." Holiness is the descent of divinity into the midst of our concrete world—"For the Lord thy God walketh in the midst of thy camp . . . therefore shall thy camp be holy" (Deut. 23:15)—it is the "contraction" of infinity within a finitude bound by laws, measures, and standards, the appearance of transcendence within empirical reality, and the act of objectification and quantification of that religious subjectivity that flows from hidden sources. Now, however, in the light of the idea of creation stored up in the treasure-house of Halakhah, this outlook on holiness takes on additional dimensions. The dream of creation finds its resolution in the actualization of the principle of holiness. Creation means the realization of the ideal of holiness. The nothingness and naught, the privation and the void are rooted in the realm of the profane; the harmonious existence, the perfected being are grounded in the realm of the holy. If a man wishes to attain the rank of holiness, he must become a creator of worlds. If a man never creates, never brings into being anything new, anything original, then he cannot be holy unto his God. That passive type who is derelict in fulfilling his task of creation cannot become holy. Creation is the lowering of transcendence into the midst of our turbid, coarse, material world; and this lowering can take place only through the implementation of the ideal Halakhah in the core of reality (the realization of the Halakhah=contraction=holiness=creation).

But man himself symbolizes, on the one hand, the most perfect and complete type of existence, the image of God, and, on the other hand, the most terrible chaos and void to reign over creation. The contradiction that one finds in the macrocosm between ontic beauty and perfection and monstrous "nothingness" also appears in the microcosm—in man—for the latter incorporates within himself the most perfect creation and the most unimaginable chaos and void, light and darkness, the abyss and the law, a coarse, turbid being and a clear, lucid existence, the beast and the image of God.[115] All human thought has grappled with this strange dualism that is so pronounced in man and has sought to overcome it. From Plato and Aristotle, who distinguished between the nutritive soul, the sensitive soul, and the rational soul, to the psychoanalytic school of Freud and his followers, who sought to probe the depths of man's subconscious, this problem of dualism keeps reappearing and demanding its resolution.

Judaism declares that man stands at the crossroads and wonders about the path he shall take. Before him there is an awesome alternative—the image of God or the beast of prey, the crown of creation or the bogey of existence, the noblest of creatures or a degenerate creature, the image of the man of God or the profile of Nietzsche's "superman"—and it is up to man to decide and choose.[116] "'Thou didst fashion me after and before' (Ps. 139:5)—R. Ishmael b. Tanhum said: After all the actions and before all the punishments. If he proves worthy, we say to him you preceded creation, as it is written: 'And the spirit of God [i.e., man] hovered over the face of the waters' (Gen. 1:2); but, if not, a gnat preceded you, a snail preceded you."[117] Herein is embodied the entire task of creation and the obligation to participate in the renewal of the cosmos. The most fundamental principle of all is that man must create himself. It is this idea that Judaism introduced into the world.

III

THE Halakhah introduced the concept of creation, in all its force and splendor, into both the commandment of repentance and the fundamental principles of providence, prophecy, and choice.

Repentance, according to the halakhic view, is an act of creation—self-creation. The severing of one's psychic identity with one's previous "I," and the creation of a new "I," possessor of a new consciousness, a new heart and spirit, different desires, longings, goals—this is the meaning of that repentance compounded of regret over the past and resolve for the future.

"If a person transgressed any of the commandments of the Torah . . . then when he repents and turns away from his sin, he is obliged to confess before God, blessed be He. . . . So, too, those who have to bring sin offerings or guilt offerings, when they bring their offerings for sins committed in error or willfully, do not obtain atonement through those offerings until they have repented and made a verbal confession, as it is written: 'He must confess the sin he has committed' (Lev. 5:5). So, too, those sentenced to death by the court and those sentenced to lashes do not obtain atonement through death or lashes until they have repented and confessed. So, too, one who injures his fellow man or damages his property, even though he pays what he owes him, does not obtain atonement until he confesses and turns aside from ever again acting in such a manner."[118] On the one hand, Maimonides is of the opinion that *viddui*, verbal confession, is an indispensable part of the act of repentance. "He does not obtain atonement until he confesses and repents." On the other hand, we find the following statement in the Baraita: "[If a man says to a woman: 'Be thou betrothed unto me] on condition that I am righteous,' even if he is absolutely wicked she is betrothed, for he may have had thoughts of repentance in his heart." Moreover, Maimonides codifies this law in *Hilkhot Ishut* [Laws of Marriage].[119] We see from here that verbal confession is not an indispensable part of repentance, and that the mere thought of repentance suffices. This contradiction requires examination. But in truth the Halakhah has posited two separate laws, two distinct principles,[120] with reference to repentance and its function. (1) Repentance may serve to divest the sinner of his status as a *rasha*, a wicked man. (2) Repentance may serve as a means of atonement like other means of atonement—sacrifices, the Day of Atonement, afflictions, death, and such like. The lack of verbal confession prevents repentance only from serving as a means of atonement, but it does not prevent it from divesting a sinner of his status as a *rasha*. Thus if one transgresses a negative commandment, for which the penalty is lashes, excision, or the judicial sentence of death, and thereby becomes ineligible as a witness, he need not make a verbal confession in order to regain his status of eligibility, but it suffices if he simply repents inwardly through regretting his past action and resolving never to sin again. This is the law as stated in the Baraita and in Maimonides's *Hilkhot Edut* [Laws of Evidence]: "Those who are disqualified by reason of extortion or robbery, even if they subsequently make restitution, are not reinstated [as eligible witnesses] until they have repented, and remain ineligible until it is ascertained that they have reformed from their evil ways. When may usurers be considered to have reformed? When they tear up their notes of their own accord. . . . When may dice players be considered to have reformed? When they voluntarily break their blocks of wood. . . . When may traffickers in the produce of the Sabbatical year be considered to have repented? When another Sabbatical year comes round and they are put to the test."[121] The sinner's regaining his status of eligibility as a witness is not at all dependent upon verbal confession, for his being divested of his status as a *rasha* has nothing to do with his obtaining atonement, but is dependent only upon the act of repentance itself consisting of regret and resolve. Repentance per se does not require verbal confession. Only the second aspect of repentance, which has as its aim the obtaining of atonement, requires verbal confession, for, as the Talmud states, "'And he shall make atonement for himself, and for his house' (Lev. 16:6): the Torah speaks of atonement through words" [Yoma 36b]. The whole function of verbal confession is limited to the realm of that repentance which serves as a means of atonement and does not penetrate into the domain of that repentance which serves to divest the sinner of his status as a *rasha*.[122]

The first principle of repentance is that the sinner be divested of his status as a *rasha*. This can only be attained if the sinner terminates his past identity and assumes a new identity for the future. It is a creative gesture which is responsible for the emergence of a new personality, a new self. This creative gesture is precipitated by an absolute decision of the will and intellect together. "What is repentance? It consists in this: that the sinner abandon his sin, remove it from his thoughts, and resolve in his heart never to repeat it . . . that he regret the past . . . and that he call the One who knows all secrets as a witness to his resolve never to return to this sin again. . . . It is also necessary that he make verbal confession and utter these matters which he had decided in his heart."[123] The abandonment of sin (i.e., the resolve for the future) and the regret over the past divest the sinner of his status as a *rasha*. They "sever" his spiritual continuity and transform his identity (and He who knows all secrets will bear witness to this act of creation). Verbal confession is directed toward precipitating the bestowal of atonement. Atonement, however, is only a peripheral aspect of repentance. Its central aspect is the termination of a negative personality, the sinner's divesting himself of his status as a *rasha*—indeed, the total obliteration of that status. "Some of the modes of manifesting repentance are that the penitent . . . change his name, as much as to say: 'I am another person and am not the same man who committed these deeds.'"[124] The desire to be another person, to be different than I am now, is the central motif of repentance. Man cancels the law of identity and continuity which prevails in the "I" awareness by engaging in the wondrous, creative act of repentance. A person is creative; he was endowed with the power to create at his very inception. When he finds himself in a situation of sin, he takes advantage of his creative capacity, returns to God, and becomes a creator and self-fashioner. Man, through repentance, creates himself, his own "I."[125]

Here there comes to the fore the primary difference between the concept of repentance in Halakhah and the concept of repentance held by *homo religiosus*. The latter views repentance only from the perspective of atonement, only as a guard against punishment, as an empty regret which does not create anything, does not bring into being anything new. A deep melancholy afflicts his spirit. He mourns for the yesterdays that are irretrievably past, the times that have long since sunk into the abyss of oblivion, the deeds that have vanished like shadows, facts that he will never be able to change. Therefore, for *homo religiosus,* repentance is a wholly miraculous phenomenon made possible by the endless grace of the Almighty.

But such is not the case with halakhic man! Halakhic man does not indulge in weeping and despair, does not lacerate his flesh or flail away at himself. He does not afflict himself with penitential rites and forgoes all mortification of body and soul. Halakhic man is engaged in self-creation, in creating a new "I." He does not regret an irretrievably lost past but a past still in existence, one that stretches into and interpenetrates with the present and the future. He does not fight the shadows of a dead past, nor does he grapple with deeds that have faded away into the distance. Similarly, his resolve is not some vacuous decision made with regard to an obscure, distant future that has not as yet arrived. Halakhic man is concerned with the image of the past that is alive and active in the center of his present tempestuous and clamorous life and with a pulsating, throbbing future that has already been "created." There is a living past and there is a dead past. There is a future which has not as yet been "created," and there is a future already in existence. There is a past and there is a future that are connected with one another and with the present only through the law of causality—the cause found at moment *a* links up with the effect taking place at moment *b*, and so on. However, time itself as past appears only as "no more" and as future appears as "not yet." From this perspective repentance is an empty and hollow concept. It is impossible to regret a past that is already dead, lost in the abyss of oblivion. Similarly, one cannot make a decision concerning a future that is as yet "unborn." Therefore, Spinoza [*Ethics* IV, 54] and Nietzsche [in *Geneaology of Morals*]—from this perspective—did well to deride the idea of repentance. However, there is a past that persists in its existence, that does not vanish and disappear but remains firm in its place. Such a past enters into the domain of the present and links up with the future. Similarly, there is a future that is not hidden behind a thick cloud but reveals itself now in all its beauty and majesty. Such a future, drawing upon its own hidden roots, infuses the past with strength and might, vigor and vitality. Both—past and future—are alive; both act and create in the heart of the present and shape the very image of reality. From this perspective we neither perceive the past as "no more" nor the future as "not yet" nor the present as "a fleeting moment." Rather past, present, future merge and blend together, and this new threefold time structure arises before us adorned with a splendid unity. The past is joined to the future, and both are reflected in the present. The principle of temporal asymmetry, of *b* following *a*, does not always serve as the distinguishing characteristic of time. Rather, a person may, not infrequently, abide in the shadow of a simultaneous past, present, and future. The law of causality, from this perspective, also assumes a new form. We do not have here the determinate order of a scientific, causal process, nor does the relationship of active cause and pre-determined passive effect prevail in such circumstances. Both "cause" and "effect" appear in an active-passive "garb"; both act and are acted upon; each influences and is influenced by the other. The future imprints its stamp on the past and determines its image. We have here a true symbiotic, synergistic relationship. The cause is interpreted by the effect, moment *a* by moment *b*. The past by itself is indeterminate, a closed book. It is only the present and the future that can pry it open and read its meaning. There are many different paths, according to this perspective, along which the cause can travel. It is the future that determines its direction and points the way. There can be a certain sequence of events that starts out with sin and iniquity but ends up with *mitzvot* and good deeds, and vice versa. The future transforms the thrust of the past. This is the nature of that causality operating in the realm of the spirit if man, as a spiritual being, opts for this outlook on time, time as grounded in the realm of eternity. However, the person who prefers the simple experience of unidimensional time—time, to use the image of Kant, as a straight line—becomes subject to the law of causality operating in the physical realm. This principle imposes the rule of the cause on the effect, the domination of an earlier point in time upon a later one.

The Halakhah declares that the person who returns to his Maker creates himself in the context of a living, enduring past while facing a bright and welcoming future. Repentance, by definition, means (1) a retrospective reflection upon the past, separating out that which is living in it from that which is dead; (2) a vision of the future in which one distinguishes between a future that is already present and one that has not as yet been "created"; (3) an examination of the cause located in the past in light of the future, determining its direction and destination. The main principle of repentance is that the future dominate the past and there reign over it in unbounded fashion. Sin, as a cause and as the beginning of a lengthy causal chain of destructive acts, can be transformed, underneath the guiding hand of the future, into a source of merit and good deeds, into love and fear of God. The cause is located in the past, but the direction of its development is determined by the future. "Great is repentance, for deliberate sins are accounted to him as meritorious deeds" [Yoma 86b]. The sin gives birth to *mitzvot*, the transgression to good deeds. In this outlook we find contained the basic principle of choice and free will. Choice forms the base of creation. Now causality and creation are two irreconcilable antagonists. If a causal lawfulness molds man's spiritual personality and points the way wherein he must go, then self-creation can have no meaning. But the above applies only if the general law of natural causality which prevails in the physical realm also operates in the world of the spirit—the cause decrees and the effect fulfills, event *a* tyrannizes over event *b*, the past is all powerful and the future must perforce follow in its wake. And it makes absolutely no difference whether the physical causality in question is mechanical in nature, as the mathematical, natural sciences founded by Galileo and Newton would have it, or teleological in nature, the view maintained by Aristotle. The only difference between Aristotle, on the one hand, and Galileo and Newton, on the other, regarding the principle of causality, is a directional one. While the mechanical view sees the cause as the beginning of a process and looks for it outside the effect, the teleological view locates the cause at the end of the process, existing within its effect. However, both outlooks admit that the effect is predetermined by the cause and that there can be no change in the direction of influence. Therefore, the creative gesture, of which man is capable, cannot be reconciled with the scientific concept of causality, whether it be prospective or retrospective. But it can be reconciled with the principle of causality that is rooted in the type of time consciousness we described earlier. When the future participates in the clarification and elucidation of the past—points out the way it is to take, defines its goals, and indicates the direction of its development—then man becomes a creator of worlds. Man molds the image of the past by infusing it with the future, by subjecting the "was" to the "will be." To be sure, each cause gives rise to a new causal sequence. But this sequence can oftentimes head in various directions. It stands at the crossroads and ponders: Whither? If man so desires, it will travel in the direction of eternity; the past will heed his word and attach itself to him. The causes will submit to his directives. The idea of the reign of the future over the past is, no doubt, highly paradoxical, but it is the no less true for all that. The life of the individual and the community confirms this fact. A great man can utilize his past sins and transgressions for the sake of achieving great and exalted goals. "In the place where repentant sinners stand, even the wholly righteous cannot stand" [Berakhot 34b; Maimonides, *Laws of Repentance* 7:4]. Historical crimes, past aberrations, can, at times, descend upon dry bones like the life-giving dew of resurrection, to which world history so amply testifies.

IV

THE experience of halakhic man is not circumscribed by his own individual past but transcends this limited realm and enters the domain of eternity. The Jewish people's all-embracing collective consciousness of time—the sages of the tradition, the Second Temple era, the age of classical prophecy, the revelation on Mount Sinai, the Exodus from Egypt, the lives of the patriarchs, the creation itself—is an integral part of the "I" awareness of halakhic man. His time is measured by the standard of our Torah, which begins with the creation of heaven and earth. Similarly, halakhic man's future does not terminate with the end of his own individual future at the moment of death but extends into the future of the people as a whole, the people who yearn for the coming of the Messiah and the kingdom of God. The splendor of antiquity and the brilliance of the eschaton envelop halakhic man's time consciousness. We have here a blurring of the boundaries dividing time from eternity, temporal life from everlasting life. Spinoza, in order to introduce the idea of eternity (*sub quadam aeternitatis specie*) into the highest conception of the world afforded by knowledge, divested being of the attribute of time and ascribed to it only the attribute of space, extension. Judaism declares: There can be no eternity without time. On the contrary, everlasting life only reveals itself through the medium of the experience of time—the hour is transformed into infinity, the moment into eternity. Man can glimpse eternity only through the consciousness of time. The whole thrust of the various commandments of remembrance set forth in the Torah—for example, the remembrance of the Exodus, the remembrance (according to Nahmanides) of the revelation at Mount Sinai [see Nachmanides's critical glosses on Maimonides, *Book of Commandments*, "Negative commandments not included by Maimonides: No. 2"], the remembrance of the Sabbath day (through the recitation of the *kiddush*), the remembrance of Amalek—is directed toward the integration of these ancient events into man's time consciousness. The Exodus from Egypt, the divine revelation on Mount Sinai, the creation of the world, all are transformed into an integral part of the content of man's present consciousness, into a powerful, direct experience. The commandment to relate the story of the Exodus carries with it a unique halakhah: "In every generation a man must regard himself as if he came forth out of Egypt" [Pesahim 10:5; cf. Maimonides, *Laws of Hametz and Matzah* 7:6]. But how can a person regard himself as one of those who left Egypt, as a companion of Moses and Aaron in the remote dawn of our history, if not by including himself in this ancient past and in the process of redemption that occurred then? But these remembrances are not just tied up with the past; they also point the way to the infinite future. The redemption from Egypt is linked to the future redemption. This connection is drawn in the blessings of *emet ve-yatziv* and *emet ve-emunah* immediately following the morning and evening *Shema*, respectively. Similarly, we conclude the *seder* on Passover night by reciting *Hallel*, the great *Hallel*, and *Nishmat*, all of which speak of the Scriptural vision of the eschaton. The revelation on Mount Sinai foreshadows the perfection of the world under the kingdom of the Almighty, when His glory will be revealed unto all. The text of the blessing *Shofarot* [Rams' horns] in the Musaf prayer of Rosh Ha-Shanah bears witness to this connection. The blessing begins with verses describing the revelation of the Torah on Mount Sinai and concludes with verses depicting the sounding of the *shofar* of the Messiah and the future redemption of Israel. The remembrance of Amalek symbolizes Israel's battle against the hosts of wickedness and the arrogant kingdom until the coming of the Messiah. "This day, on which was the beginning of Thy work, is a memorial for the first day." This is the prayer of the Jewish people on Rosh Ha-Shanah [from the blessing *Zikhronot* (Remembrances) in the Musaf prayer of Rosh Ha-Shanah]. They celebrate the anniversary of the creation of the world. This metaphysical act is still embedded in the nation's consciousness, as they pray on that very day for the renewal of the cosmos. The infinite past enters into the present moment. The fleeting, evanescent moment is transformed into eternity. But the covenantal community, daughter Zion, continues thus her supplications before the King sitting in judgment: "Our God and God of our fathers, reign over the whole universe in Thy glory, be exalted over all the earth in Thy grandeur" [from the blessing *Malkhuyot* (Kingships) in the Musaf prayer of Rosh Ha-Shanah]. Not only the infinite past but also the infinite future, that future in which there gleams the reflection of the image of eternity, also the splendor of the eschatological vision, arise out of the present moment, fleeting as a dream. Temporal life is adorned with the crown of everlasting life.

"Moses received the Torah from Sinai, and transmitted it to Joshua," etc. [Avot 1:1]. This is the motto of the Halakhah. The *masorah*, the process of transmission, symbolizes the Jewish people's outlook regarding the beautiful and resplendent phenomenon of time. The chain of tradition, begun millennia ago, will continue until the end of all time. Time, in this conception, is not destructive, all-consuming, and it does not simply consist of fleeting, imperceptible moments. This wondrous chain, which originated on that bright morning of the day of revelation and which stretches forward into the eschaton, represents the manner in which the Jewish people experience their own history, a history that floats upon the stormy waters of time. The consciousness of halakhic man, that master of the received tradition, embraces the entire company of the sages of the *masorah*. He lives in their midst, discusses and argues questions of Halakhah with them, delves into and analyzes fundamental halakhic principles in their company. All of them merge into one time experience. He walks alongside Maimonides, listens to R. Akiva, senses the presence of Abaye and Raba. He rejoices with them and shares in their sorrow. "David, king of Israel, yet lives and endures" [Rosh Ha-Shanah 25a]; "Our father Jacob did not die" [Ta'anit 5b; cf. Gen. Rabbah 96:4]; "Moses, our teacher, did not die" [Zohar I, 37b]. There can be no death and expiration among the company of the sages of tradition. Eternity and immortality reign here in unbounded fashion. Both past and future become, in such circumstances, ever-present realities.

In truth, the dualism bound up with the concept of time has been well known since Bergson. The distinction between the concept of mathematical time, frozen in geometrical space and entirely quantifiable, and the perception of time as pure, qualitative duration, forming the very essence and content of consciousness and streaming ever onward (and only the act of memory can enable one somehow to grasp hold of this rushing stream), was largely responsible for the rebellion of the human sciences (*geisteswissenschaften*) against the methodology of the mathematical, natural sciences. Nowadays, philosophy operates with a dual conception of time: (1) mathematical-physical time; (2) historical time. The former is being quantified in ever-increasing measure (its quantitative nature has been emphasized most strikingly by the union of space and time in the theories of Minkowski and Einstein), while the latter, from day to day, is apprehended more and more as pure quality. All of the investigations of the phenomenological school into the nature of time have as their aim elucidating its qualitative character. Similarly, the special nature of causality in the realm of the spirit (psychic-historical causality) occupies an important place in modern philosophy.

The Halakhah, however, is not particularly concerned with the metaphysics of time. Moreover, it is not inclined to transform time into pure, flowing, evanescent quality. Judaism disapproves of too much subjectivity, of an undue emphasis on quality. Therefore, it does not view time from the perspective of the *geisteswissenschaften*. The fact that the concept of time in the Halakhah is bound up with measurable time periods—days, weeks, months, years, sabbatical and jubilee cycles—demonstrates that Judaism does not desire a flowing stream of time but rather wishes to establish a time that is fixed and determined.[126]

The fundamental principle of the halakhic outlook on time is practical and ethical in nature.

We have already emphasized earlier that man is given the choice of deciding between two perceptions of time—evanescence and eternity—and ordering his life accordingly.

There is a kind of person who seeks refuge in the shadow of a fragmented, shattered time. He frequents a present that has cut itself off from the past and the future and finds itself in the narrow four cubits of the fleeting moment. The antinomy contained in the idea of time—"The past already gone by, the future not yet nigh, the present, the blink of an eye" [a popular medieval adage]—appears here in all its terror. Yesterday has already passed, tomorrow is yet to come, and today rapidly descends into the abyss of oblivion. Such a man is subject to the general scientific law of causality—the cause rooted in the past determines the image of the future. His existence does not enjoy the blessings of liberty and free will. The yesterday creates both the now and the tomorrow, and all three deride and mock him. Actions long since gone precipitate deeds yet to come. Life is out of his control. He can create neither himself nor his future. There is no psychic continuity here, only an existence completely out of joint. Continuity, by definition, means the future imprinting its stamp upon the past. However, when today and tomorrow are dominated and controlled by yesterday, that spiritual constancy whose content is a never-ending process of self-creation simply disappears. Such a life the sages called *ḥayyei sha'ah*, temporal life.

But there is a kind of man who abides under the shadow of a complete and resplendent time. His soul, grounded "in days past" (Deut. 4:32), in the early history of his people, is devoted to the eschatological ideal. He looks behind him and sees a hylic matter that awaits the reception of its form from the creative future. He looks ahead of him and confronts a creative, shaping force that can delineate the content of the past and mold the image of the "before." He participates in the unfolding of the causal sequence and the ongoing act of creation. He views existence from the perspective of eternity and enjoys the splendor of creation. His consciousness embraces the entire historical existence of the Jewish people. Such a time consciousness, whose beginning and end is everlasting life, is the aim of Halakhah and is termed creation—the realization of the eternal Halakhah in the very midst of the temporal, fleeting world, the "contraction" of the glory of the infinite God in the very core of concrete reality, the descent of an everlasting existence into a reality circumscribed by the moment. Not for naught does Judaism speak of (1) the world as a finite entity;

(2) the world under the aspect of eternity and infinity. A coincidence of opposites? Nevertheless! In the midst of finitude there appear traces of infinity; in the midst of the fleeting moment an ever-enduring eternity. The symbol of this outlook is the idea of repentance, which is identical with true creation.[127]

V

THE old problem of the status of the individual, which had its roots in the philosophy of Aristotle and which, for a long time, engaged the attention of the Christian and Arab scholastics, found both its clearest expression and its most profound and original solution in the philosophy of Maimonides. Obviously, the view of Averroës, that only the universal active intellect is immortal and not the individual passive intellect, contradicts the very foundations of Judaism. Maimonides disagreed with this view, as did Albertus Magnus and Thomas Aquinas after him.[128] Nevertheless, the whole question of the immortality of the soul, particularly as it relates to the individual passive intellect (the hylic or potential intellect), is a very difficult and important one, and here Maimonides appears in his full intellectual and ethical splendor as he resolves this problem in a brilliant and striking fashion.

On the one hand, Maimonides subscribed to the view of Aristotle (and Plato)[129] that true, authentic existence is to be found only in the realm of the forms—the universal ideas— while the realm of particularity, rooted in matter (as an individuating principle) does not attain the level of complete being but exists only as an image of the universal. On the other hand, the Halakhah has always insisted upon the principle of individual immortality. How can these two apparently contradictory positions be maintained?

This same problem reappears in the discussion surrounding the issue of providence. For certainly the belief in individual providence is a cornerstone of Judaism, both from the perspective of the Halakhah and from the perspective of philosophical inquiry. It is the tenth of Maimonides's thirteen fundamentals of faith.[130] The protagonist of the religious drama, according to Judaism, is the individual, responsible for his actions and deeds, and there can be no responsibility or accountability without providence. Therefore, Maimonides placed man in a special category by himself, distinct from that of all other creatures, and proclaimed that man's own particular existence as an individual is of significance, both with reference to the principle of immortality and the principle of individual providence. "As for my own belief with regard to this fundamental principle, the meaning of divine providence, it is as I shall set it forth to you. In the belief that I shall set forth, I am . . . relying upon what has clearly appeared as the intention of the book of God and of the books of our prophets. . . . For I believe that in this lowly world—I mean that which is beneath the sphere of the moon—divine providence watches only over the individuals belonging to the human species and that in this species all the circumstances of the individuals and the good and evil that befall them are consequent upon their deserts, just as it says: 'For all His ways are justice' (Deut. 32:4). But regarding all the other animals and, all the more, the plants and other things, my opinion is that of Aristotle. . . . For all these texts [asserting that there is providence over animals] refer to providence watching over the species and not to individual providence. . . . It does not follow for me that by virtue of this opinion one may pose to me the following question—namely: Why does He watch over the human individuals and not watch in the same way over the individuals belonging to the other species of animals? For he who propounds this question ought to ask himself: Why did He give intellect to man and not to the other species of animals? The answer to this last question is: He willed it so."[131]

The gist of Maimonides's view is that man occupies a unique

position in the kingdom of existence and differs in his onto-logical nature from all other creatures. With reference to all other creatures, only the universal, not the particular, has a true, continuous existence; with respect to man, however, it is an everlasting principle that his individual existence also at-tains the heights of true, eternal being. Indeed, the primary mode of man's existence is the particular existence of the individual, who is both liable and responsible for his acts. Therefore, it is the individual who is worthy of divine provi-dence and eternal life. Man, in one respect, is a mere random example of the biological species—species man—an image of the universal, a shadow of true existence. In another respect he is a man of God, possessor of an individual existence. The difference between a man who is a mere random example of the biological species and a man of God is that the former is characterized by passivity, the latter by activity and creation. The man who belongs solely to the realm of the universal is passive to an extreme—he creates nothing. The man who has a particular existence of his own is not merely a passive, recep-tive creature but acts and creates. Action and creation are the true distinguishing marks of authentic existence.

However, this ontological privilege, which is the peculiar possession of the man who has a particular existence of his own, a privilege that distinguishes him from all other creatures and endows him with individual immortality, is dependent upon man himself. The choice is his. He may, like the indi-vidual of all the other species, exist in the realm of the images and shadows, or he may exist as an individual who is not a part of the universal and who proves worthy of a fixed, established existence in the world of the "forms" and "intellects separate from matter" [Maimonides, *Laws of the Foundations of the Torah* 4:9]. Species man or man of God, this is the alternative which the Almighty placed before man. If he proves worthy, then he becomes a man of God in all the splendor of his individual existence that cleaves to absolute infinity and the glorious "divine overflow." If he proves unworthy, then he ends up as one more random example of the biological species, a turbid and blurred image of universal existence.[132] "According to me, as I consider the matter, divine providence is consequent upon the divine overflow and the species with which this intellectual overflow is united. . . . But I believe that providence is consequent upon the intellect and attached to it. For providence can only come from an intelligent being, from one who is an intellect perfect with a supreme perfection. . . . Accordingly, everyone with whom something of this overflow is united will be reached by providence to the extent to which he is reached by the intellect. . . . When any individual has obtained, because of the disposition of his matter and his training, a greater portion of this overflow than others, providence will of necessity watch more carefully over him than over others—if, that is to say, providence is, as I have mentioned, consequent upon the intellect. Accordingly, divine providence does not watch in an equal manner over all the individuals of the human species, but providence is graded as their human perfection is graded. . . . It follows necessarily that His providence, may He be exalted, that watches over the prophets is very great and proportionate to their degree in prophecy and that His providence that watches over excellent and righteous men is proportionate to their excellence and righteousness. For it is this measure of the overflow of the divine intellect that makes the prophets speak, guides the actions of the righteous men, and perfects the knowledge of the excellent men with regard to what they know. As for the ignorant and disobedient, their state is despicable proportionately according to their lack of this overflow, and they have been relegated to the ranks of the individuals of all the other species of animals: 'He is like the beasts that speak not' (Ps. 49:13, 21)."[133]

Man, at times, exists solely by virtue of the species, by virtue of the fact that he was born a member of that species, and its general form is engraved upon him. He exists solely on account of his participation in the idea of the universal. He is just a member of the species "man," an image of the universal. He is just one more example of the species image in its ongoing morphological process (in the Aristotelian sense of the term). He himself, however, has never done anything that could serve to legitimate his existence as an individual. His soul, his spirit, his entire being, all are grounded in the realm of the universal. His roots lie deep in the soil of faceless mediocrity; his growth takes place solely within the public domain. He has no stature of his own, no original, individual, personal profile. He has never created anything, never brought into being anything new, never accomplished anything. He is receptive, passive, a spiritual parasite. He is wholly under the influence of other people and their views. Never has he sought to render an accounting, either of himself or of the world; never has he examined himself, his relationship to God and his fellow man. He lives unnoticed and dies unmourned. Like a fleeting cloud, a shadow, he passes through life and is gone. He bequeaths nothing to future generations, but dies without leaving a trace of his having lived. Empty-handed he goes to the grave, bereft of *mitzvah* performances, good deeds, and meritorious acts, for while living he lacked any sense of historical responsibility and was totally wanting in any ethical passion. He was born involuntarily, and it is for this reason and this reason alone that he, involuntarily, lives out his life (a life which, paradoxically, he has "chosen"!) until he dies involuntarily. This is man as the random example of the biological species.

But there is another man, one who does not require the assistance of others, who does not need the support of the species to legitimate his existence. Such a man is no longer a prisoner of time but is his own master. He exists not by virtue of the species, but solely on account of his own individual worth. His life is replete with creation and renewal, cognition and profound understanding. He lives not on account of his having been born but for the sake of life itself and so that he may merit thereby the life in the world to come. He recognizes the destiny that is his, his obligation and task in life. He understands full well the dualism running through his being and that choice which has been entrusted to him. He knows that there are two paths before him and that whichever he shall choose, there must he go. He is not passive but active. His personality is not characterized by receptivity but by spontaneity. He does not simply abandon himself to the rule of the species but blazes his own individual trail. Moreover, he, as an individual, influences the many. His whole existence, like some enchanted stream, rushes ever onward to distant magical regions. He is dynamic, not static, does not remain at rest but moves forward in an ever-ascending climb. For, indeed, it is the living God for whom he pines and longs. This is the man of God.

The fundamental of providence is here transformed into a concrete commandment, an obligation incumbent upon man. Man is obliged to broaden the scope and strengthen the intensity of the individual providence that watches over him. Everything is dependent on him; it is all in his hands. When a person creates himself, ceases to be a mere species man, and becomes a man of God, then he has fulfilled that commandment which is implicit in the principle of providence.

VI

THE most exalted creation of all is the personality of the prophet. Each man is obligated to give new life to his own being by modeling his personality upon the image of the prophet; he must carry through his own self-creation until he actualizes the idea of prophecy—until he is worthy and fit to receive the divine overflow. The principle of prophecy, as an article of faith, like the fundamental of providence, has a twofold aspect: the belief in (1) prophecy as a reality—i.e., that God causes men to prophesy; (2) prophecy as a norm—i.e., that each person is obliged to aspire to this rank, that every man should make a supreme effort to scale the mountain of the Lord, until he reaches the pinnacle of the revelation of the Divine Presence. Thus, the belief in prophecy has an ethical and practical dimension; it incorporates within its scope binding and authoritative law. Prophecy is man's ultimate goal, the end point of all his desires. "It is one of the foundations of religion to know that God causes men to prophesy. Prophecy rests only on an exceedingly wise man, who is strong with respect to his moral habits so that his inclination [yetzer] does not overcome him in anything whatsoever but he, through the use of his mind, always overcomes his inclination, and who also possesses an exceedingly broad and ready mind. A person who is endowed with all these moral habits and who is physically sound, when he enters the *pardes* [the "garden" of the divine science] and pursues those great and distant matters, and he possesses a mind that is ready for understanding and comprehending, and he sanctifies himself and withdraws from the path of the generality of the people who walk in the darkness of the times, for he prods himself and teaches his soul not to take any thought at all of any empty matters nor of the vanities of the age and its contrivances, his mind always facing upward, bound beneath the [celestial] throne, to understand the holy, pure forms, and to behold the wisdom of the Holy One, blessed be He, in its entirety, from the first form until the center of the earth, and to know from them His greatness—at once, the Holy Spirit rests upon him."[134] Maimonides incorporated in this halakhah, which deals with the fundamental of prophecy— i.e., "that God causes men to prophesy"—a description of the personality and spiritual stature of the prophet. And with good reason. For the image of the prophet and the structure of his consciousness are also parts of the principle of prophecy; they serve both as man's "telos" and as the ideal of ethical perfection, as posited by Halakhah. "The sixth fundamental is that of prophecy—i.e., that a man should know that among the species of man there are to be found men whose nature is such that they possess exalted and refined moral habits and great perfection, and their souls are ready until they finally receive the form of the intellect. Afterward the human [acquired] intellect will cleave to the active intellect, and there will over-flow from the active intellect onto the human intellect a mighty overflow. These are the prophets and this is prophecy."[135] Maimonides, in the above passage, explicitly states that the fundamental of prophecy includes two elements: (1) the per-sonality of the prophet; (2) the phenomenon of prophecy. To be sure, the outpouring of the spirit, the divine overflow, is dependent upon heavenly grace; nevertheless, the prepara-tion for prophecy and the task of self-creation have been entrusted to man.[136]

When a person reaches the ultimate peak—prophecy—he has fulfilled his task as a creator. "At once the Holy Spirit rests upon him. And when the Spirit descends upon him, his soul commingles with the rank of the angels called *ishim* [viz., the active intellect] and he is turned into another person. And he will understand that he is not the same as he had been, but that he has been elevated above the rank of the other wise men, even as it is said of Saul: 'And thou shalt prophesy with them, and shalt be turned into another man' (1 Sam. 10:6)."[137] The prophet creates his own personality, fashions within himself a new "I" awareness and a different mode of spiritual existence, snaps the chains of self-identity that had linked him to the "I" of old—to man who was just a random example of the species, who "walk[ed] in the darkness of the times"—and turns into a man of God, his mind "bound beneath the [celestial] throne." In sum, the task of creation with which man is charged is, according to the Halakhah, a triple performance; it finds its expression in the capacity to perform *teshuvah,* to repent, con-tinues to unfold in *hashgaḥah,* the unique providence which is bestowed upon the unique individual, and achieves its final and ultimate realization in the reality of prophecy and the personality of the prophet. Man starts with repentance, with a fleeting awareness of sin, with the feeling of regret for the past and determination for the future; he continues to exercise his creative powers by searching for individual providence to single him out as an independent personality; and he finally closes and consummates the cycle of creation with attaining the level of prophecy. This is the path that the Halakhah has charted for man to travel.

The mystery of creation, according to Maimonides, is latent in the adhesion of the initially passive intellect—which functions with reference to the active intellect as does matter in its potentiality with reference to the form that acts upon it—to the active intellect. Man initially is receptive, is pure potentiality. But creation, by definition, means spontaneity, actuality, action, renewal, aspiration, and daring. Therefore, man must become a creature that both acts and causes others to act. The potentiality must transform itself into actuality, the receptivity into spontaneity. The hyle in this process of creation must ultimately be able to act, drawing upon its own resources. The creature must become a creator, the object who is acted upon a subject who acts. The concept of the individual action is of major importance in Judaism, and this idea molds the shape of the concept of creation as it appears in Maimonides's philosophy. Moreover, Maimonides's view on this matter is consistent with his overall philosophical system. Cognition, for Maimonides, is the identity of the intellect, the intellectually cognizing subject and the intellectually cognized object. Moreover, for Maimonides, this principle of identity not only applies to the infinite, divine cognition but also to finite, human cognition.[138] The moment the hylic intellect (the material intellect, as it is called by the Arab philosophers, or passive intellect, as it is termed by the Aristotelians) passes from potentiality to actuality—i.e., at the moment of actual cognition—it unites and conjoins with the active intellect. However, this identity is constant and eternal only with respect to the infinite divine intellect but not with respect to the intellects of His creatures, for their cognition is finite and intermittent. The identity is broken when the act of cognition ceases. As long as the act of cognition lasts, the unity remains in force. For this reason the great ideal of man is to multiply acts of intellectual cognition (in frequent succession) in order thereby firmly to establish (to be sure, with many interruptions, for is not the absolute continuity of cognition reserved solely for God?) the constancy of the unifying act of cognition. Man has the choice to devote his hylic intellect either to the apprehension of the senses and the imagination, which is restricted to matter circumscribed by space and time, or to a pure intellectual cognition of the separate, essential forms.[139] Creation finds its expression in man's fulfilling all of his tasks, causing all of the potentiality implanted in him to emerge into actuality, utilizing all of his manifold possibilities, and fully bringing to fruition his own noble personality. The power stored up within man is exceedingly great, is all-encompassing, but all too often it slumbers within and does not bestir itself from its deep sleep. The command of creation, beating deep within the consciousness of Judaism, proclaims: Awake ye slumberers from your sleep. Realize, actualize yourselves, your own potentialities and possibilities, and go forth to meet your God. The unfolding of man's spirit that soars to the very heavens,[140] that is the meaning of creation.

In truth, Greek philosophy was also familiar with the notion of a process of development from relative nothingness to a perfect existence. What is more, this problem is practically the central issue in Greek ontology. The dispute between Heraclitus and Parmenides concerning the nature of being—whether it is perpetual development and movement or fixed, perfect existence—still made itself felt in the analyses of the Platonic and Aristotelian schools and their successors. Aristotle's idea of the fourfold nature of existence was an attempt to solve this problem. Two out of the four ontic aspects of existence represent, on the one hand, the ultimate, complete being, pur⸤ actuality (as conceived by Parmenides), and, on the other hand, potential reality—the prime hylic matter—which in truth, according to Aristotle, does not have any real existence of its own (but is only an abstraction). Between these two poles there is the realm of movement in which one finds the coming into being of existence and the entire process of development (as pictured by Heraclitus). There is an ever-ascending hierarchy of matter and form, at the top of which is thought thinking itself (νόησις νοήσεως). Existence (apart from the first form), by definition, means development, the passing from potentiality into actuality. The process of development from possibility (δύναμις) to entelechy (ἐντελέχεια) is the fundamental principle of reality.[141]

However, a vast abyss separates the view of Aristotle from the ontological outlook of Maimonides, the master halakhist, this despite the fact that the latter uses the terms of the former with respect to this question. First, the whole concept of creation never really took hold in Greek philosophy. As a result of this, Greek philosophy had no room for the true creative act. In its stead it posited an ever-unfolding, necessary concatenation of events.[142] Such a process of development cannot be transformed into an ethical principle, a norm and obligation binding upon man. The pure, first form does not create; therefore, man is not obliged to create.

Second, the eudaemonistic ideal (the search for happiness), which serves for Aristotle as the highest ethical good, cannot inspire man to create. Neither the intellectual virtues of Aristotelian ethics nor the aspiration for the contemplative life (βίος θεωρητικός) are in any way equivalent with the yearning for creation that has so entirely seized hold of the Jewish imagination. The longing for the theoretical life does not consist so much in the realization within the realm of one's own individuality of the potentiality that is latent in matter, as in the abstracting of form from matter. The desire of the theoretical type, according to the view of Plato, Aristotle, and the Stoics, is directed toward complete abstraction and absolute union with the perfect, ultimate realm of universality. The dream of the Attic sage is the obliteration of that particularity which is rooted in matter. Individuality simply cannot exist in the world of a Greek philosopher from any of these schools.

Judaism, however, is grounded in its awareness of and esteem for the individual. "He who preserves a single life it is as though he preserved an entire world" [Sanhedrin 4:6]. Judaism seeks to fortify, strengthen, and ground the reality of the individual, to elevate him to exalted ontological heights. The individual is redeemed by the Halakhah precisely because it leaves the philosophical realm far behind and is thereby able to shape man's personality by means of the new idea of creation which it has introduced to the world. The realm of the universal exists from the very beginnings of creation; the realm of the particular is created by man himself.

The concept of creation has its roots in the Halakhah, and from there it was transferred by Maimonides to the domain of philosophy. Therefore, Maimonides, in the *Mishneh Torah*, used the Aristotelian notions of active and passive intellect very sparingly but instead took up at great length the new principle which Judaism brought to light—namely, prophecy as a binding ethical ideal, prophecy as an act of self-creation and self-renewal.

The concept of creation sheds a clear light on the fundamental principle of choice and free will. This principle expresses itself on two levels: (1) man is free to create himself as a man of God; he has the ability to shatter the iron bars of universality and strict causality that imprison him qua man as a random example of the species; (2) this man of God, fashioned and created by man himself, having shattered that structured lawfulness governing the species, is no longer under its dominion and need not heed its dictates. He exists in his own private domain; he lives a free, autonomous, individual, and unique existence. The teleological law of the species no longer

exerts any power over him. Now we know that Maimonides
accepted the Aristotelian view that lawfulness is primarily an
inner teleological process[143] whereby the form of the species is
actualized in the individual. Therefore, as long as man has not
ascended to the rank of existence where he leaves behind him
the domain of the universal and enters into his own personal
domain—no longer dependent upon the principles operative
in the realm of the universal—he is still subject to the rule of
the species and the universal form. However, as soon as he
liberates himself from the burden of the species, he becomes a
free man. Complete freedom belongs only to the prophet, the
man of God. The man who is a mere random example of the
species, on the other hand, is wholly under the rule of the
scientific lawfulness of existence. Between this species man
and the man of God, between necessity and freedom, is
the middle range in which most people find themselves.
Some ascend in the direction of complete freedom; others
descend in the direction of complete servitude. Man, initially,
must cause all of the potentialities of the species implanted
in him to pass into actuality; he must completely realize
the form of the species "man."[144] However, once he has
actualized this universal form, then, instead of having his
own specific image obliterated, he acquires a particular form,
an individual mode of existence, a unique personality and
an active, creative spirit. He leaves behind the domain of
the species and enters his own personal domain. The realization of the universal in man's being negates any claim
that the species has on him. This outlook is truly striking
in its paradoxical nature. It is a hybrid of two views: the
view of Aristotle, with its emphasis on the universal, and
the view of the Halakhah, with its emphasis on the individual. The method is Greek, the purpose halakhic. The
goal of self-creation is individuality, autonomy, uniqueness,
and freedom. However, as was explained earlier, the complete freedom of the man of God is embodied in his percep-

tion of the norm as an existential law of his own individual and spiritually independent being; he discovers his freedom in the halakhic principle, which is deeply rooted in his pure soul. For this norm, this principle is unaccompanied by any sense of compulsion, and a person does not feel "as though he were compelled by some mysterious, hidden power." Rather he rejoices in its fulfillment and realization.

In this light we can understand why Maimonides broadened the principle of choice to encompass man's entire spiritual being (rather than limiting it solely to the question of will). Man's spirit is free and independent. It is not subject to the lawful structure of the universal, to the necessity of the species. The "universal" in the existence of the man of God is free from the chains of scientific lawfulness, for it was created in accordance with the principle of freedom and is wholly grounded in that principle.

"Choice is granted to every human being. If a man wants to follow the good path and be good, the choice is his; if he wants to follow the evil path and be wicked, the choice is his. . . . Let it not occur to your mind that God decrees at the birth of a person that he shall be good or evil, a notion expressed by foolish non-Jews and the multitude of ignorant Jewish individuals. It is not so. Every human being is fit to become as righteous as Moses or as wicked as Jeroboam, wise or foolish, merciful or cruel, niggardly or generous; and so with all other traits."[145] Indeed, man's entire spiritual existence is enhanced by his unique privilege to create himself and make himself into a free man. The voluntaristic motif finds its full expression here, for in the final analysis it is the will which is the source of freedom. Therefore, when the will expands to the far reaches of man's being, it takes the entire spiritual world in its sweep and reigns over it in unbounded fashion. The triumph of freedom in the realm of the spirit testifies to the dominion and influence of the will on all the other manifestations of man's inner experience. More power and strength to the will! Now we have already emphasized earlier that, for Maimonides, the cosmos is an expression of the will of the Almighty. God created the world for the sake of His will. Therefore, when God apportioned some of His glory to mortal man and bestowed upon him the power of creation, He grounded this creative power in man's will. The will outwits the structured lawfulness of the species; it creates a new, free mode of being in man, one which is not enslaved by the rule of the structured lawfulness of the universal but which it ascends to the very heavens and cleaves to the divine overflow. The will is the source of repentance, providence, prophecy, and the freedom of the spirit. However, this whole process of development unfolds in an ethical-halakhic spirit. The intellect, the will, feeling,[146] the whole process of self-creation,[147] all proceed in an ethical direction.

And halakhic man, whose voluntaristic nature we have established earlier, is, indeed, a free man. He creates an ideal world, renews his own being and transforms himself into a man of God, dreams about the complete realization of the Halakhah in the very core of the world, and looks forward to the kingdom of God "contracting" itself and appearing in the midst of concrete and empirical reality.

These are but some of the traits of halakhic man. Much more than I have written here is imprinted in his consciousness. This essay is but a patchwork of scattered reflections, a haphazard collection of fragmentary observations, an incomplete sketch of but a few of halakhic man's features. It is devoid of scientific precision, of substantive and stylistic clarity. Indeed, it is an indifferent piece of work. But it is revealed and known before Him who created the world, that my sole intention was to defend the honor of the Halakhah and halakhic men, for both it and they have oftentimes been attacked by those who have not penetrated into the essence of Halakhah and have failed to understand the halakhic personality. And if I have erred, may God, in His goodness, forgive me.

Notes

1. Obviously the description of halakhic man given here refers to a pure ideal type, as is the case with the other types with which the human sciences (*geisteswissenschaften*) are concerned. Real halakhic men, who are not simple but rather hybrid types, approximate, to a lesser or greater degree, the ideal halakhic man, each in accordance with his spiritual image and stature. See Eduard Spranger, *Lebensform geistesswissenschaftliche Psychologie und Ethik der Personlichkeit* (Halle, 1922) [*Types of Man*, trans. P. J. W. Pigors (Halle, 1928)].

2. See Ferdinand Lassalle, *Die Philosophie Herakleitos des Dunklen von Ephesos* [Berlin, 1858; repr. in *Gessamelte Reden und Schriften*, ed. E. Bernstein, vols. 7 and 8 (Berlin, 1920)]; and Georg Brandes's book on Lassalle [*Ferdinand Lassalle* (London/New York, 1911), pp. 32–41]. Lassalle's contention that there is an accord between Heraclitus's philosophy and that of Hegel has not been accepted by historians of Greek philosophy.

3. The father of dialectical or crisis theology.

4. Even though Kierkegaard disagreed with Hegel's philosophy from beginning to end and made it the object of his fierce, stinging attacks, he, nevertheless, accepted from him the dialectical principle (with many significant changes, to be sure). And this concept of the dialectic, which he and Karl Barth introduced into the analysis of the unfolding of the religious consciousness, and this view concerning the antinomic structure of religious experience, which was revised and refined by Rudolf Otto in his book, *The Idea of the Holy,* give the lie to the position that is prevalent nowadays in religious circles, whether in

Protestant groups or in American Reform and Conservative Judaism, that the religious experience is of a very simple nature—that is, devoid of the spiritual tortuousness present in the secular cultural consciousness, of psychic upheavals, and of the pangs and torments that are inextricably connected with the development and refinement of man's spiritual personality. This popular ideology contends that the religious experience is tranquil and neatly ordered, tender and delicate; it is an enchanted stream for embittered souls and still waters for troubled spirits. The person "who comes in from the field, weary" (Gen. 25:29), from the battlefield and campaigns of life, from the secular domain which is filled with doubts and fears, contradictions and refutations, clings to religion as does a baby to its mother and finds in her lap "a shelter for his head, the nest of his forsaken prayers" [H. N. Bialik, "Hakhnisini taḥat kenafekh"] and there is comforted for his disappointments and tribulations. This ideology is partially embedded in the most ancient strata of Christianity, partially rooted in modern pragmatic philosophy; but mainly it stems from practical-utilitarian considerations. The advocates of religion wish to exploit the rebellious impulse against knowledge which surges from time to time in the soul of the man of culture, the yearning to be freed from the bonds of culture, that daughter of knowledge, which weighs heavy on man with its questions, doubts, and problems, and the desire to escape from the turbulence of life to a magical, still, and quiet island and there to devote oneself to the ideal of naturalness and vitality. This Rousseauean ideology left its stamp on the entire Romantic movement from the beginning of its growth until its final (tragic!) manifestations in the consciousness of contemporary man. Therefore, the representatives of religious communities are inclined to portray religion, in a wealth of colors that dazzle the eye, as a poetic Arcadia, a realm of simplicity, wholeness, and tranquillity. Most of the sermons of revivalists are divided in equal measure between depicting the terrors of hellfire and describing the utopian tranquillity that religion can bestow upon man. And that which appears in the sermons of these preachers in a primitive, garbled form, at times interwoven with a childish naïveté and superficial belief, is refined and purified in the furnace of popular "philosophy" and "theology" and becomes transformed into a universal religious ideology which proclaims: If you wish to acquire tranquillity without paying the price of spiritual agonies, turn unto religion! If you wish to achieve a fine psychic equilibrium without having to first undergo a slow, gradual personal development, turn unto religion. And if you wish to achieve an instant spiritual wholeness and simplicity that need not be forged out of the struggles and torments of consciousness, turn unto religion! "Get thee out of thy country," which is filled with anxiety, anguish, and tension, "and from thy birthplace," which is so frenzied, raging, and stormy, "to the land" that is enveloped by the stillness of peace and tranquillity, to the Arcadia wherein religion reigns supreme. The leap from the secular world to the religious world could not be simpler and easier. There is no need for a process of transition with all its torments and upheavals. A person can acquire spiritual tranquillity in a single moment. Typical of this attitude is the Christian Science movement.

It would appear to me that there is no need to explain the self-evident falsity of this ideology. First, the entire Romantic aspiration to escape from the domain of knowledge, the rebellion against the authority of objective, scientific cognition which has found its expression in the biologistic philosophies of Bergson, Nietzsche, Spengler, Klages, and their followers and in the phenomenological, existential, and antiscientific school of Heidegger and his coterie, and from the midst of which there arose in various forms the sanctification of vitality and intuition, the veneration of instinct, the desire for power, the glorification of the emotional-affective life and the flowing, surging stream of subjectivity, the lavishing of extravagant praise on the Faustian type and the Dionysian personality, etc., etc., have brought complete chaos and human depravity to the world. And let the events of the present era be proof! The individual who frees himself from the rational principle and who casts off the yoke of objective thought will in the end turn destructive and lay waste the entire created order. Therefore, it is preferable that religion should ally itself with the forces of clear, logical cognition, as uniquely exemplified in the scientific method, even though at times the two might clash with one another, rather than pledge its troth to beclouded, mysterious ideologies that grope in the dark corners of existence, unaided by the shining light of objective knowledge, and believe that they have penetrated to the secret core of the world.

And, second, this ideology is intrinsically false and deceptive. That religious consciousness in man's experience which is most profound and most elevated, which penetrates to the very depths and ascends to the very heights, is not that simple and comfortable. On the contrary, it is exceptionally complex, rigorous, and tortuous. Where you find its complexity, there you find its greatness. The religious experience, from beginning to end, is antinomic and antithetic. The consciousness of *homo religiosus* flings bitter accusations against itself and immediately is filled with regret, judges its desires and yearnings with excessive severity, and at the same time steeps itself in them, casts derogatory aspersions on its own attributes, flails away at them, but also subjugates itself to them. It is in a condition of spiritual crisis, of psychic ascent and descent, of contradiction arising from affirmation and negation, self-abnegation and self-appreciation. The ideas of temporality and eternity, knowledge and choice (necessity and freedom), love and fear (the yearning for God and the flight from His glorious splendor), incredible, overbold daring, and an extreme sense of humility, transcendence and God's closeness, the profane and the holy, etc., etc., struggle within his religious consciousness, wrestle and grapple with each other. This one ascends and this descends, this falls and this rises.

Religion is not, at the outset, a refuge of grace and mercy for the despondent and desperate, an enchanted stream for crushed spirits, but a raging, clamorous torrent of man's consciousness with all its crises, pangs, and torments. Yes, it is true that during the third Sabbath meal at dusk, as the day of rest declines and man's soul yearns for its Creator and is afraid to depart from that realm of holiness whose name is Sabbath, into the dark and frightening, secular workaday week, we sing the psalm "The Lord is my shepherd; I shall not want. He maketh me to lie down in green pastures; He leadeth me beside the still waters" (Ps. 23), etc., etc., and we believe with our entire hearts in the words of the psalmist. However, this psalm only describes the ultimate destination of *homo religiosus*, not the path leading to that destination. For the path that eventually will lead to the "green pastures" and to the "still waters" is not the royal road, but a narrow, twisting footway that threads its course along the steep mountain slope, as the terrible abyss yawns at the traveler's feet. Many see "the Lord passing by; and a great and strong wind rending mountains and shattering rocks . . . and after the wind an earthquake . . . and after the earthquake a fire" but only a few prove worthy of hearing "the still small voice" (1 Kings 19:11–12). "Out of the straits have I called, O Lord" (Ps. 118:5). "Out of the depths I have called unto Thee, O Lord" (Ps. 130:1). Out of the straits of inner oppositions and incongruities, spiritual doubts and uncertainties, out of the depths of a psyche rent with antinomies and contradictions, out of the bottomless pit of a soul that struggles with its own torments I have called, I have called unto Thee, O Lord.

And when the Torah testified that Israel, in the end, would repent out of anguish and agony [cf. Maimonides, *Laws of Repentance* 7:5], "In your distress when all these things are come upon you . . . and you will return unto the Lord your God" (Deut. 4:30), it had in mind not only physical pain but also spiritual suffering. The pangs of searching and groping, the tortures of spiritual crises and exhausting treks of the soul purify and sanctify man, cleanse his thoughts, and purge them of the husks of superficiality and the dross of vulgarity. Out of these torments there emerges a new understanding of the world, a powerful spiritual enthusiasm that shakes the very foundations of man's existence. He arises from the agonies, purged and refined, possessed of a pure heart and new spirit. "It is a time of agony unto Jacob, but out of it shall he be saved" (Jer. 30:7)—i.e., from out of the very midst of the agony itself he will attain eternal salvation and redemption. The spiritual stature and countenance of the man of God are chiseled and formed by the pangs of redemption themselves.

5. One of the thirteen rules for interpreting the Torah is the contradiction between two verses and their harmonization by a third verse. Therefore, it is not for naught that the Midrash (Gen. Rabbah 56:8 [cited in Rashi on Gen. 22:12]) informs us that after the angel told Abraham, "Lay not thy hand upon the lad, neither do thou any thing unto him" (Gen. 22:12), Abraham arose and asked: Yesterday You told me "For in Isaac shall seed be called to thee" (Gen. 21:12), and today You told me "Take now, thy son, thine only son . . . and offer him there for a burnt-offering" (Gen. 22:2), etc., etc.—i.e., the exalted drama of the *Akedah*, of the binding of Isaac, is reflected not only in the act of self-sacrifice on the part of the father and the son and in the offering up of Isaac as a sacrifice on the altar, but also in the struggle taking place within Abraham's soul. For it seemed to him as though the words of God were contradictory, heaven forbid; nevertheless, he overcame the pangs and torments of contradiction, rose up early in the morning and saddled his ass. When the angel appeared to him and revealed to him the third verse which harmonized the two contradictory verses, then Abraham rose up and questioned. I once heard from my father [R. Moses Soloveitchik] in the name of our great master, R. Hayyim of Brisk [R. Soloveitchik's paternal grandfather], that as long as the third harmonizing verse had not yet been revealed, Abraham had no right to question God's word, and for this reason he contained himself until the end of the epic. The pangs of consciousness of the man of God and the towering and awesome strength of his self-restraint shine forth here in a clear and pure light.

6. Neither the question of the nature of the metaphysical and noetic impulse of cognitive man, which has been extensively discussed by many philosophers—from Aristotle to present-day scholars—nor

the problem of the teleological thrust of cognition which is so prevalent in contemporary philosophy affects in any way the notion of the structure and the aim of cognition.

7. Modern philosophy of religion recognizes that there are cognitive aspects to the religious act. A precise analysis of the religious experience gives the lie to all the schools which denied the noetic stance of *homo religiosus*.

8. The circumference of a circle=$2 \pi r$.

9. The area of a circle= πr^2.

10. The concept of the absolute (the thing in itself—*Das Ding an sich*), the Achilles' heel of Kant's philosophy, in truth is not a spiritual offspring of cognitive man (*Die reine vernunft*) but rather of a murky religiosity. Cognitive man does not speak about the "existence" of a thing whose content and nature he cannot determine. Such an approach is one of the basic characteristics of *homo religiosus*. Solomon Maimon and Hermann Cohen, both of whom were influenced by the mathematical, natural sciences, omitted the absolute from their philosophies. An object which cannot be apprehended by cognitive man is of no concern to philosophy. However, there is a profound paradox in the philosophies of Maimon and Cohen. On the one hand they deleted the absolute from the world view of cognitive man, while on the other hand they created through this omission an exaggerated doctrine of idealism which subjects reality to cognition possessed of an absolute character, and epistemological idealism itself is imbued with a religious tinge, as will be explained later.

11. The neo-Kantian school set the problem and the goal in the center of its philosophy, which understands cognition as a dynamic process (a Hegelian concept, except that Hegel understood the movement of the logos in a dialectical manner). The *Fieri* [thing to be done] in the place of the *Factum* [thing which has been done] and the *Actus* [that which is to be effected] in the place of the *Actum* [that which has been effected] obviously result in placing the goal and the problem in the very core of the doctrine. However, the neo-Kantian goal differs entirely from the goal of cognition of God, as set forth in the philosophy of Maimonides. For the neo-Kantians, the problem does not express itself in concealing and hiding but rather in creating and revealing. The process of cognition does not conceal, but creates and discloses. Both the problem itself and the unending task (*Die unendliche Aufgabe*) constitute an essential part of the process of the unfolding and "creation" of the logos, for is it not the case that there is no existence without cognition? Even in Hermann Cohen's first period

[his commentaries on Kant's three critiques], when the absolute (*Das Ding an sich*) still appeared—to be sure only qua task (*Aufgabe*) and not qua given (*Gegebenheit*)—the riddle which surpasses cognition did not enter into his rationalist outlook. How much more so is it the case with his later writings [his three systematic works of philosophy: *Logic of Pure Cognition; Ethics of Pure Will; Aesthetics of Pure Feelings*], where any idea of the absolute (even qua task) has disappeared, that the incomprehensible does not enter into the charmed circle of his philosophy. *Homo religiosus* "senses" a problem that was not created by the logos but that exists eternally without any relationship to cognition. The religious riddle is transcendent, sealed, and opaque.

12. Even though this saying is not to be found in any of his extant writings, it symbolizes Tertullian's stance excellently.

13. [Laws of the Foundations of the Torah 1:1, 6.] Cf. Maimonides, Positive Commandment 1, *Book of Commandments* [Berlin, 1914; 2d rev. ed. (New York/New Jersey, 1946)], edited by my friend, the Gaon, light of the Diaspora, R. Hayyim Heller, may he enjoy a long and good life [now of blessed memory], and his note ad loc. Similarly cf. *Avodat ha-melekh* [(Vilna, 1931); repr. (Jerusalem, 1971); on *Laws of the Foundations of the Torah* 1:1], by my uncle, Rabbi M. Krakowski.

14. I do not wish to become embroiled in the midst of the dispute regarding the nature of negative apprehension according to Maimonides, whether it is plain *Docta ignorantia* or whether it is affirmative in its essence, for there are outstanding scholars ranged on both sides of this question. Many have already discussed this matter (Hermann Cohen in his essay on Maimonides ["Characteristik der Ethik Maimunis," *Jüdische Schriften*, vol. 3 (Berlin, 1924), pp. 248–259, trans. into Hebrew by Zvi Wissolowsky, "Ofyah shel torat ha-middot le-ha-Rambam," in *Iyyumin be-yahadut U-ve-ba'ayot ha-dor* (Jerusalem, 1977), pp. 33–40]; David Kaufman in his great work *Geschichte der Attributenlehre in der jüdischen Philosophie des Mittelatters von Saadja bis Maimuni* [(Gotha, 1877), pp. 428–470]; David Neumark [*Toldot ha-filosofiyah be-Yisrael*, vol. 2: *Homer ve-tzurah* (Matter and form) (Philadelphia, 1929), pp. 367, 372], Julius Guttman [*Die Philosophie des Judentums* (Munich, 1933), pp. 182–186; *Ha-filosfiyah shel ha-yahadut* (Jerusalem, 1951), pp. 149–153; *Philosophies of Judaism*, trans. D. W. Silverman (New York, 1964), pp. 159–165]; and others. See Judah [Even-Shmuel] Kaufmann's notes to his edition of the *Guide of the Perplexed* [vol. 1:2 (Tel Aviv, 1938), pp. 26 ff., in particular p. 26, n. 67, and his commentary on *Guide* I, 50–60]). This question does not at all affect the matter under discussion. In any event the affirmative cognition of existence—

the attributes of action—is prior to negative cognition. See *Laws of the Foundations of the Torah* 2:1, 2 and the *Guide* I, 54. The cognition of the Creator is possible, according to Maimonides's view, only through the cognition of the attributes of action—i.e., this vast and great cosmos. As a result of this cognition we arrive at the negation of the essential attributes.

15. See *Laws of the Foundations of the Torah* 1:9–12; 2:1, 2, 10; *Laws of Repentance* 5:5; 8:2.

16. Like the approach of Fichte, which, from the standpoint of cognitive man, is cognitive-normative.

17. The positivist doctrine, from David Hume to Ernst Mach, Richard Avenarius, and the circle of pragmatists that clustered around William James, with all of the transformations and changes it underwent, typifies this approach.

18. The idealist understanding of the autonomous process of cognition (which is rooted in classical rationalism) from Kant to Hermann Cohen and his disciples, symbolizes this view in all its rich variety of colors and hues. I am using this analogy in order to make the whole subject of halakhic man more palatable to scholars of religion who are not familiar with this type. Therefore, I shall not enter into a detailed discussion of this central problem. I will not, for the present, discuss the views of the positivist and pragmatist schools, which I mentioned above, regarding mathematics and the mathematical natural sciences. I desire only to elucidate the nature of halakhic man by drawing upon the philosophical understanding of mathematics as an a priori science which deals with ideal constructions. This view is prevalent not only in all the doctrines that have been influenced by Kantian and neo-Kantian philosophy but also within the circles of great contemporary mathematicians and physicists.

Even the phenomenological school, which is sharply critical of Kantianism and its innovations, concedes the ideal nature of the mathematical object. However, it rejects the whole concept of the construction of mathematics. For is not the ideal nature of essentiality (*essentia*) absolute and fixed, in which case it was not created by thought? It is open to a unique type of understanding which the phenomenologists term the intuition of essences (*Wesenschau*).

19. See Tosafot, Menaḥot 66a, s.v. *zekher le-mikdash hu;* Maimonides, *Laws of Daily and Additional Offerings* 7:22, 23; *Shulḥan Arukh: Oraḥ Ḥayyim* 489:3, 7.

20. Shabbat 34b.

21. Pesaḥim 58a.

22. See *Malbushei yom tov* [by R. Lipele of Mir, vol. 2 (Vilna, 1892)]: *Kuntrus hovat karka* [chaps. 14–16, pp. 22–28] for a discussion of the legal standard of formation of fruits or leaves (*hanitah*).

23. According to the interpretation of the Rashbam, contra the interpretation of Rabbenu Tam [see Bava Batra 35a].

24. When epistemological doctrine speaks of the a priori nature of mathematics, it is not approaching the subject from a psychogenetic vantage point but rather from the perspective of a systematic, transcendental outlook concerning the nontemporal nature of mathematical knowledge and its inherent necessity and truth. This approach is particularly exemplified by the transcendental method of Kant as interpreted by the philosophy of Hermann Cohen.

25. Sanhedrin 71a.

26. Kiddushin 40b: "Now the question was put before them: Is study greater, or is practice greater? ... R. Akiba replied: Study is greater, for study leads to practice. R. Jose said: Study is greater for it preceded the law of *hallah* by forty years and the laws of the tithes and heave offerings by fifty-four years." See Tosafot, ad loc.

27. R. Raphael Ha-Kohen of Hamburg [1722–1803] devoted an entire work, *Ve-shav ha-kohen* [Altona, 1792], to the sacrificial laws. R. Aryeh Leib b. Asher Günzburg of Metz [1695–1785] devoted almost his entire work *Gevurot ha-ari* on Yoma [published posthumously, 1902] to the sacrificial laws. Similarly, in his classic works *Turei even* [Metz, 1781] and *Sha'agat aryeh* [Frankfort on the Oder, 1755], he takes great delight and intense pleasure in subjecting even those laws that are not practiced nowadays to acute halakhic analysis. R. Isaac of Karlin delved deeply into the whole area of sacrificial law in his series of novella on the Talmud, *Keren orah* (for example, on Menahot [Warsaw, 1884], Nazir [Vilna, 1869], etc.). The work *Mei nifto'ah* [by R. Judah Edel (Bialystok, 1816)], which was constantly at the side of R. Hayyim Soloveitchik of Brisk, consists of a commentary on Maimonides's *Introduction to the Laws of Purities* [in his Commentary on the Mishnah]. The success of the halakhic work *Minhat hinukh* [by R. Joseph Babad (1800–1875), published in 1869 and reprinted many times] is, in large measure, owing to the fact that the author did not limit himself to discussing family and civil law but concerned himself with all the commandments of the Torah. On the contrary, the author only touched briefly on matters of civil law but discussed at length those laws that were operative only when the Temple was still standing. The halakhic work *Or Sameiah* [Dvinsk, 1902–1926] of R. Meir Simha Ha-Kohen of Dvinsk [1843–1926] encompasses the entire

Torah. A substantial portion of my father's halakhic manuscripts are also devoted to problems of sacrificial law. I content myself with citing only a few isolated examples, "for should I string out a list like some peddler enumerating his wares?" [a Talmudic image; see Gittin 32b, Bava Kamma 36b].

28. *Laws of Creditor and Debtor* 15:1–2.

29. *Laws of Loans and Deposits* 5:5–6.

30. *Laws of Hiring* 2:3.

31. *Likkutei amarim* of R. Shneur Zalman of Lyady, [pt. I, chap. 5, pp. 9a–b].

32. The yearning of halakhic man to actualize the ideal idea is reflected in the prayer of the holiday Musaf service: "Because of our sins we were exiled from our land. . . . We cannot go up as pilgrims to worship Thee, to perform our duties in Thy chosen house, the great and holy Temple. . . . May it by Thy will to bring us unto Zion, Thy city. . . . There will we prepare in Thy honor our obligatory offerings. . . ."

33. Later on we will elaborate upon this yearning of halakhic man for the complete realization of this ideal construction in this world, and we will emphasize that this longing is the central idea of Judaism.

34. The only dead person for whom the high priest and the Nazarite must defile themselves is a *meit mitzvah*—i.e., a dead person who has no relatives to take care of his burial.

35. See Tosafot, Berakhot 18a, s.v. *le-mahar;* Tosafot, Bava Batra 74a, s.v. *paski hada karna di-tekhelta;* Tosafot, Niddah 61b, s.v. *aval oseh; Tur, Yoreh De'ah* and *Shulhan Arukh, Yoreh De'ah* 351.

36. With reference to whether other offerings are accepted [by God] if they are brought after the donor's death, see Zevahim 5b–6a, where the Gemara concludes that such offerings do not effect a fixed [absolute] atonement but do make a "floating" atonement. Similarly, note carefully Maimonides's statement, *Laws of Daily and Additional Offerings* 3:22: "If the high priest died in the morning after he offered the half-tenth and another high priest was not appointed in his stead, the heirs bring a whole tenth to make atonement for him." Cf. Sifrei, piska 210 on *kapeir le-amkha Yisrael* (Deut. 21:8) and the critical gloss of R. Moses Isserles, *Shulhan Arukh, Orah Hayyim* 621:6.

37. *Laws of Sabbath* 2:3.

38. See Mo'ed Katan 15b; Tosefta Zevahim 11:1; Maimonides, *Laws of Entrance into the Sanctuary* 2:11.

39. See *Laws of the Temple Vessels* 5:6: "He does not rend his garments over his dead [relative]. . . . And if he did rend them, he is to

be flogged. Nor may he let his hair grow long at any time . . . for it is said, 'He shall not let the hair of his head grow long' (Lev. 21:10) even when he is not entering the sanctuary." This statement of Maimonides would seem to imply that the prohibition against the high priest's letting his hair grow long is not restricted to the case where he lets his hair grow long in mourning for his dead relative; however the prohibition against the high priest's rending his garment applies only if he rends his garment over his dead relative. But in the *Laws of the Defilement of Leprosy* 10:6 (see Mo'ed Katan 15) Maimonides states that the law which requires a high priest who has become a leper to let his hair grow long and rend his garment is based upon the principle that a positive commandment overrides a negative commandment. This would seem to imply that both prohibitions, the prohibition forbidding the high priest to let his hair grow long and that forbidding him to rend his garments, are not just restricted to a high priest who lets his hair grow long or rends his garments in mourning over his dead, but are generally applicable. See Maimonides's *Book of Commandments*, Negative Commandment no. 164, *Sefer ha-ḥinukh*, Commandments nos. 149, 150, and the Commentary of the *Minḥat ḥinukh*, ad loc. [s.v., *ve-kefel ha-meni'a ba mipnei tosefet davar*].

40. Maimonides (*Laws of Mourning* 7:5–6) obligates the high priest to observe all the laws of mourning [with the exception of rending his garments and letting his hair grow long]. Cf. however Mo'ed Katan 14b where Raba states: "A high priest during the year is on a par with any other person on a festival." [This would seem to imply that a high priest should not observe any of the laws of mourning just like an ordinary person does not observe any of the laws of mourning during a festival.] This problem has been thrashed out by the more recent authorities. See *Keren orah* on Mo'ed Katan, ad loc., and *Minḥat ḥinukh* on Commandment no. 264.

41. How different is this view from that of Plato regarding bodily existence as it comes to the fore in his dialogue *Phaedo* and indeed from the general Greek attitude regarding the conjoining of body and soul, an attitude that resulted in the negation of the body. See Reinhold Neibuhr, *The Nature and Destiny of Man* (New York, 1941), vol. 1, chap. 1, ["The Classical View of Man"].

42. See Shevu'ot 13b: "If a person ate a piece of meat [on the Day of Atonement] and choked on it so that he died" [even Rabbi who says that the Day of Atonement bestows atonement for sins committed on the day itself would admit that the sinner in this instance would incur *karet*, would be cut off]. Tosafot, ad loc., states: "The Talmud does not

necessarily mean that the person must have choked on the meat [in order not to receive atonement], for the same law would apply as long as the person [who ate the meat] died before the end of the day." Thus, the Tosafists are of the opinion that the end of the day atones. [Therefore, if the person died before the end of the day, he does not receive atonement for his sin.] Rashi, however, states: "He committed his sin [until his death] so that not even one moment of the day elapsed after his sin." His view is that the entire day atones. [Therefore, if even one moment of the day elapsed from the time the person committed the sin of eating until his death, that moment would bestow atonement for his sin.] See Rashba, ad loc.

43. Bava Metzia 86a.

44. Midrash Tanḥuma Ḥukkat, s.v. *ve-yikḥu elekha* (Num. 19:2).

45. Avodah Zarah 3b.

46. See above, note 4.

47. Maimonides, *Hilkhot Talmud Torah* 3:1. Cf. Yoma 72b and R. Hannanel ad loc.

48. Maimonides, *Commentary on the Mishnah*: introduction to chap. Ḥelek, "Thirteen Principles of Faith: Fifth Principle." Cf. *Laws of Repentance* 3:5, 7; *Laws of Idolatry* 1:1.

49. Similarly they skip the piyyut "Angels of mercy."

50. See Rudolf Otto, *Das Heilege* [*The Idea of the Holy,* trans. J. Harvey (London, 1950)].

51. See Hermann Cohen, *Religion der Vernunft aus den Quellen des Judentums* [(Frankfurt, 1919), trans. into Hebrew by Zvi Wissolovsky, *Dat ha-tevunah mi-mekorot ha-yahadut* (Jerusalem, 1971), and trans. into English by S. Kaplan, *Religion of Reason out of the Sources of Judaism* (New York, 1972)] and Moritz Lazarus, *Die Ethik des Judentums* [2 vols. (1898–1911), vol. 1 trans. into English from the manuscript by Henrietta Szold, *Ethics of Judaism,* 2 vols. (Philadelphia, 1900–1901)]. The distinction that Lazarus introduced between ethical holiness and ritual holiness, a distinction which was accepted as self-evident by the school of German-Jewish philosophers (including Hermann Cohen), is a figment of Lazarus's imagination that fits in with the world view of liberal religious Judaism, which based Judaism upon ethics.

52. Cf. Exod. Rabbah 15:24: "'This new moon shall be unto you the beginning of months' (Exod. 12:2). What blessing was to be recited by one who beheld the new moon in the period when Israel used to sanctify the new months? . . . Some rabbis hold: [He recited] 'Who sanctifies Israel'—since unless Israel sanctifies it, it is not sanctified at all. . . . And because they are sanctified unto God, therefore all that

they sanctify is sanctified. . . . God said: 'I am sanctified, do I then need sanctification? But I will sanctify Israel so that they might sanctify me.'"

53. The tones of the idea of macrocosm-microcosm are echoing here.

54. I am not discussing here the concept of *tzimtzum* in the kabbalistic literature in general; rather I am making use of the interpretation of this concept to be found in the teachings of Habad Hasidism [i.e., the teachings of R. Shneur Zalman of Lyady].

55. See *Likkutei Torah* (Vilna, 1928), *Nitzavim*, p. 44c passim.

56. Ibid.

57. Maimonides, *Laws of the Foundation of the Torah* 2:10.

58. Now it has already been explained above . . . [concerning] the flow from the light of the *Ein-Sof* [the infinite], blessed be He . . . that a new light flows from the source of the *Ein-Sof*, blessed be He, through [the medium of] His goodness—i.e., [God] in the aspect of "abundant grace" (Exod. 34:6). . . . For [with respect to God] in His essence, may He be blessed, it has been stated "For I the Lord, change not" (Mal. 3:6) and [therefore] no attributes at all apply to Him. Therefore, that there should be a flow and revelation from the *Ein-Sof* in His aspect of wise . . . is a great descent [for Him], and [it is only] through His grace,— as it is stated "The world is built upon grace" (Ps. 89:3)—that He lowers Himself so that He may be termed "wise." *Likkutei Torah: Song of Songs* on "I am black, but comely" (Songs 1:5), p. 9b.

59. "For the wailing is for the distance [separating the individual] from the *Ein-Sof*, may He be blessed, in His revealed aspect. . . . For there are many, mighty contractions, tens of thousands unfathomable levels. . . . And when the *maskil* [the wise, discerning individual] ponders this distance from the revealed light of the *Ein-Sof*, may He be blessed, and how many contractions and worlds conceal the revelation of the light of the *Ein-Sof*, blessed be He, the source of delight . . . he breaks out into prolonged wailing." *Likkutei Torah, Nitzavim*, p. 48a.

60. *Likkutei Torah, Nitzavim*, p. 44c.

61. Even from the perspective of God as He who fills all worlds, the world only exists from one vantage point. The attribute of *tzimtzum* expresses itself in two ideas: concealment and disclosure. On the one hand, God sustains the cosmos through concealing and hiding His glory, and were He to reveal Himself, then all would revert to chaos and the void, for who can withstand the splendor of His excellence when He comes forth to overawe the earth? [See Isa. 2:19, 21.] It is the concealment of the Divine countenance which brings into being all existence. On the other hand, the Almighty gives life to and sustains all

existence through the disclosure of His glory, for He is the root and source of reality, and the concealment of the Divine countenance would result in the destruction of the world and the negation of reality. Only the act of disclosure creates. This powerful antinomy, "splendid in its holiness," is practically the central axis of Habad doctrine. Concealment and disclosure—both equally sustain the cosmos, but both equally cause it to revert back to nothingness and naught. See *Likkutei Torah, Emor* (in the name of the Maggid of Mezeritch), p. 36b; ibid., Song of Songs on the verse "I am black, but comely" (Songs 1:5), p. 7d. This polarity is expressed by two verses: "He made darkness His screen" (Ps. 18:12) (concealment); "The Lord God is a sun and a shield" (Ps. 84:12) (disclosure).

62. This outlook is as far removed from that of the Neoplatonic school, which desires to free man from concreteness and materiality through an ecstasy which leads to dissolution into the One ($\alpha\pi\lambda\omega\sigma\iota\varsigma$), as the world view of Judaism is from that of Greek philosophy. However, this is not the place to elaborate.

63. *Guide* III, 13, 25.

64. This voluntaristic outlook influenced the philosophies of both Schopenhauer and Nietzsche. However, these thinkers distorted the voluntaristic position and thereby helped bring about the destruction of the world.

65. It is interesting that even Habad doctrine understood creation from a voluntaristic standpoint. *Keter* (the Royal Crown), which is an "intermediary" between the Emanator and the emanations, is the supernal will. See *Likkutei Torah, Song of Songs,* p. 9b, and *Likkutei amarim,* [*Iggeret ha-kodesh,* chap. 17, p. 125b; chap. 20, p. 130b]. But this entire matter is of exceptional profundity.

66. "There is yet another proper way for man to occupy himself with the Torah and commandments for their own sake. . . . It is first to arouse in his mind great mercy before God for the Divine spark which animates his soul and which has descended from its source, the life of life, the *Ein-Sof,* blessed be He, who fills all worlds and encompasses all worlds and in comparison with whom all is accounted as naught. Yet [this spark] has clothed itself in a 'serpent's skin' and is at the greatest possible remove from the King's countenance, since this world is the nether point of the coarse *kelipot* (husks). . . . And this is the secret [doctrine] of the exile of the *Shekhinah.*" *Likkutei amarim* [I, 45, pp. 64a–b].

67. Rosh Ha-Shanah 31a.

68. Gen. Rabbah 19:7.

69. Num. Rabbah 13:2.

70. *Likkutei amarim, Iggeret ha-kodesh*, [chap. 10, p. 115a].

71. See the statement of *Likkutei amarim* cited above.

72. *Guide* I, 59.

73. See H. N. Bialik's essay "Halakhah ve-aggadah" [in *Kol kitvei Bialik* (Tel Aviv, 1951), pp. 207-214].

74. Maimonides's ruling is not clear. See *Laws of Recitation of Shema* 2:1; *Laws of Hametz and Matzah* 6:3; *Laws of Shofar* 2:4-5; *Laws of Megillah* 2:5.

75. *Nodeh bi-Yehudah* [of R. Ezekiel Landau]: *Yoreh De'ah, Mahdurah Kamma*, Responsum no. 93; cf. *Orah Hayyim, Mahdurah Tinyana*, Responsum no. 107.

76. See *Likkutei Torah: Derashot le-Rosh Ha-Shanah*, pp. 55b-57a.

77. Rosh Ha-Shanah 33b.

78. Maimonides, *Laws of Lulav* 8:12.

79. And the question of values and teleology in modern epistemological theory does not change this fact.

80. This concept of freedom should not be confused with the principle of ethical autonomy propounded by Kant and his followers. The freedom of the pure will in Kant's teaching refers essentially to the creation of the ethical norm. The freedom of halakhic man refers not to the creation of the law itself, for it was given to him by the Almighty, but to the realization of the norm in the concrete world. The freedom which is rooted in the creation of the norm has brought chaos and disorder to the world. The freedom of realizing the norm brings holiness to the world. See Hermann Cohen, "Das Problem der jüdischen Sittenlehre: Eine Kritik von Lazarus' Ethik des Judentums" [*Jüdische Schriften*, vol. 3, pp. 1-36].

81. "If man is worthy, they say to him: 'You preceded the ministering angels'; but if he is unworthy, they say to him: 'A gnat preceded you, a snail preceded you'" (Gen. Rabbah 8:1).

82. See Max Scheler, *Die Stellung des Menschen im Kosmos* (Bern, 1928) [*Man's Place in Nature*, trans. Hans Meyerhoff (Boston, 1960); cf., as well, Scheler, "*Mensch und Geschichte*" in *Philosophische Weltanschauung* (Bonn i Cohen, 1929)]; Reinhold Niebuhr, *The Nature and Destiny of Man* [vol. 1, chaps. 7-8, "Man as Sinner," pp. 178-240].

83. See below regarding this dualism.

84. Judaism does not agree with the view of Christian theologians, who see in pride the source of all sin and iniquity. Even though it also hates pride, it nevertheless did not take an extreme position on this issue. See Maimonides, *Laws of Moral Dispositions* 1:1-5. Similarly, read

carefully R. Bahya ibn Pakuda, *Duties of the Heart,* chap. 6, "On Humility." The many statements of the sages that strongly denigrate pride do not, in any event, consider it to be the supreme fount of all sins.

85.　Eruvin 13b. See below for our elucidation of the concept of repentance.

86.　See Stefan Zweig, "Tolstoy," *Drei Dichter ihres Lebens* [*Adepts in Self-Portraitures,* trans. Eden and Cedar Paul (New York, 1928), p. 238]. Zweig writes that Tolstoy conquered the fear of death that had seized hold of him through an act of objectification—i.e., transforming death into an object of his artistic creation.

87.　The one exception to this rule is the cognition of God. On the contrary, when man cognizes the Creator of the cosmos, he submits himself more and more to His infinite will. It is from thence that there arises the aura of mystery that surrounds the cognition of God, which the doctrine of negative attributes discerned. However, this is not the place to elaborate.

88.　See William James, *The Varieties of Religious Experience* [lectures 6 and 7, "The Sick Soul"].

89.　Maimonides, *Laws of Mourning* 13:11.

90.　This is not the place to engage in lengthy comparisons between the stance of halakhic man concerning the pangs and sorrows of existence and the views of the Stoics and Epicureans regarding this matter.

91.　Bava Metzia 59b.

92.　Maimonides, *Law of the Foundations of the Torah* 9:4. See, [however], Bava Metzia 59b; Tosafot, ad loc., s.v. *lo ba-shamayim hi;* Zevahim 62a; *Laws of the Sanctuary* 2:4; Eruvin 13b.

93.　Deut. Rabbah 2:14.

94.　Exod. Rabbah 15:30; cf. Exod Rabbah 30:9.

95.　R. Hayyim Volozhin, *Ruah hayyim,* Commentary on Avot [6:1, p. 34b].

96.　"This is the meaning of the verse 'And God created man in His image, in the image of God created He him' (Gen. 1:27) . . . that just as He, may His name be blessed, is God (*Elohim*)—i.e., the master of all the forces in all of the worlds—and He orders and guides the actions of these worlds at every moment in accordance with His will, so He, in accordance with His will, gave man dominion so that he might control myriads of forces and worlds in accordance with the particulars of the order of his actions in all of his affairs at literally each and every moment, as determined by the supernal roots of his actions, words, and thoughts, as though he, too, were their master as it were [*Nefesh ha-ḥayyim* 1:3 (p. 2a)]. . . . And this idea is alluded to in the statement of the sages in Avot: 'Know that which is higher *mimkha* [than you or from you]'—i.e., even though you cannot see with your vision the awesome things being created by your actions, know verily that all that which is happening on high, in the very highest of worlds, is all *mimkha*, from you . . . i.e., is determined by your actions" [ibid. 1:4, note (p. 2b)]. R. Hayyim Volozhin also introduced into his world view the ancient idea of macro- and microcosmos. "However, the main point is that God created man at the very end of creation so that man should be a wondrous creature who incorporates within himself forces from all spheres, for in him are contained all the wondrous divine lights and all the supernal worlds and realms that preceded him. . . . All have imparted unto him part of themselves in his formation, and they are included in his powers [ibid. 1:6 (p. 5b)].

97. Each one discovered the calculus independent of the other.

98. See above concerning Maimonides's attitude toward piyyutim.

99. See Maimonides's introduction to the *Commentary on the Mishnah* for his interpretation of this statement.

100. *Ruaḥ ḥayyim,* commentary on Avot [6:1, pp. 34a–b]; cf. *Nefesh ha-ḥayyim* [4:2, 4:3, pp. 1b–2a].

101. See Maimonides, *Laws of Circumcision* 1:2, and the critical gloss of Rabad, ad loc.

PART TWO

102. See Zohar III, 152a. "The Torah, in all its words, holds supernal truths and divine secrets. . . . The Torah possesses a body. That body is composed of the Torah's precepts, *gufei Torah* [bodies, major principles]. The body is clothed in garments which are the narratives that relate to things of this world. The fools see only the narratives, the garments. Those somewhat more knowledgeable see also the body. But the truly wise, those who serve the most high King and stood at Mount Sinai, gaze only upon the soul [of the Torah] which is the root principle of all." Cf. Nahmanides's introduction to his *Commentary on the Torah*. "And all that was transmitted to Moses our teacher [concerning the account of creation, the account of the chariot, and the other secrets concerning man and the cosmos] through the gates of understanding, all is either written expressly in the Torah or alluded to by its words, etc."

103. Consider the statement of R. Isaac [as cited by Rashi in his commentary on Gen. 1:1]: "The Torah should have begun with the verse 'This month shall be unto you the beginning of months' (Exod. 12:2), for that is the first commandment with which Israel was commanded. What is the reason, then, that it begins with [the story of] the beginning? Because [through beginning with the account of creation] 'He hath declared to His people the power of His works [in order] to give them the heritage of the nations' (Ps. 111:6). For if the nations of the world should say to Israel, 'You are robbers, for you conquered the lands of the seven nations,' they [Israel] could reply: 'The entire world belongs to the Holy One, blessed be He; He created it and He gave it to them [to the seven nations] and of His own will He took it from them and gave it to us.'" This gives expression to the idea [of the normative significance of creation] in a somewhat different form. The thrust of this statement is that we are in need of the account of creation insofar as it functions as normative guide to halakhic practice. Cf. Nahmanides, ad loc.

104. *Sefer Ha-Yetzirah,* in fine.

105. Cf. Ḥaggigah 12a.

106. Sukkah 53a–b; Makkot 11a.

107. P. T. Sanhedrin 10:2 [29a].

108. The question as to whether the negative side of being has been in existence from the time of creation itself or whether it was precipitated by man's sin is a different problem and has no bearing upon the issue with which we are concerned. See Eruvin 18b. Cf. Gen Rabbah 2:1–5: "'Now the earth was chaos and void, and darkness was upon the face of the deep' (Gen. 1:2). R. Berekiah cited [the verse]: 'Even a child is known by his doings, whether his work be pure and whether it be right' (Prov. 20:11). R. Berekiah said: While she [the earth] was as yet immature, she produced thorns; and so the prophet was one day destined to prophesy of her, 'I beheld the earth, and, lo, it was chaos and void' (Jer. 4:23). . . . R. Tanhuma said: The earth foresaw that she was destined to meet her doom at the hand of man, as it is written, 'Cursed is the ground for thy sake' (Gen. 3:17). Therefore, the earth was *tohu* and *bohu* [i.e., bewildered and astonished]. R. Judah b. R. Simon interpreted the text ['Now the earth was chaos and void'] as referring to the generations. 'Chaos' refers to Adam who was reduced to chaos; 'and void' refers to Cain, who desired to turn the world back to void. . . . Resh Lakish applied the verse to the [various] exiles [to which Israel was subjected]. 'And the earth was chaos' refers to the Babylonian exile . . . 'upon the face of the deep' refers to the

exile [imposed by] the wicked kingdom [i.e., Rome]. . . . R. Abbahu said: 'Now the earth was chaos and void.' This alludes to the deeds of the wicked." The concept "offspring of chaos"—referring to the Amalekites [alluded to in Gen. 6:13 according to the statement in the Zohar cited below], *gibborim* (cf. Gen. 6:4), *nefilim* (cf. Gen. 6:4, Num. 13:33), *refaim* (cf. Deut. 2:11), and *anakim* (cf. Num. 13:28, 33; Deut. 1:28, 2:11)—occupies a prominent place in the Kabbalah. Cf. Ḥaggigah 13b–14a (Rashi, ad loc., s.v. *kodem she-bara ha-olam* and Tosafot, ad loc., s.v. *ve-tardan*); Zohar I, 24b–25b (on Gen. 2:4); Rabbi Isaac Nissenbaum, "*Toldin de-tohu*" [Offspring of chaos], [pp. 23–27], and "*Erev rav*" [Mixed multitude], [pp. 150–157], in *Kinyanei kedem* [Warsaw, 1931].

109. See Zohar I. 39B (on Gen. 1:2). "The first dwelling place starting from below: there is no knowledge there at all, for there is no form there at all in the imprint, etc."

110. To cite Maimonides's phrase, *Laws of the Sanctification of the New Moon* 1:6.

111. See *Guide* II, 29.

112. Shavu'ot 9a.

113. Of extreme interest is the talmudic passage (Sanhedrin 42a): "It was taught in the school of R. Ishmael: It would have sufficed had Israel merited no other privilege than to greet the presence of their Father in heaven once a month. Abaye said: Therefore we must recite it [the blessing] standing."

114. See Y. L. Peretz, *Rayze bilder: a yingl* [in Y. L. Peretz, *Bilder un skitzn* (Vilna, n.d.), pp. 43–47; trans. Helena Frank, "Travel Pictures: A Little Boy" in *Stories and Pictures* (Philadelphia, 1906), pp. 256–259]:

"The innkeeper's appealing little boy with his jerky movements and his curls, full of feathers, still haunts me. Now he stands before my eyes with a scallion in hand and he wails, he wants another; or I hear him at evening prayer saying the *kaddish* in such a childlike, plaintively earnest manner that it pierces my very heart. . . .

"Hopping on one little foot he stretches his face upward to the moon; he sighs.

"Has he seen a star fall?

"No.

"'Oh,' he says. 'How I wish the Messiah would come!'

"What?

"'I want the moon to become bigger already. It's such a pity on her. True, she sinned, but to suffer so much . . . we are already living in the sixth millennium.'

"Altogether two requests: From his father on earth, another scallion, and from his father in heaven, that the moon become bigger.

"A wild impulse seized me to tell him, 'Enough! Your father, down here, will soon get married again, soon you will have a stepmother, you will become a stepchild, and will have to wail for a piece of bread. Forgo the scallion; forget about the moon.'"

Those downtrodden and often externally unappealing *shtetl* personalities—the itinerant peddler hawking his needles, threads, and thimbles in the villages of the Pale; the plain, often coarse innkeeper; the fleshy villagers—were all nevertheless imbued with an inner bewitching attractiveness. An ember of holiness still smoldered in the hearts of these figures, who were drowning in almost overwhelming soul-crushing worries, pressures, troubles. A wondrous flame, burning in the depths of their being, lit up their desolate and oppressed spirits. On the one hand, it seemed as if all they were concerned with were the few miserable pennies and bare physical necessities they had to struggle to obtain, like that abandoned, lonely orphan boy (soon to be the object of a step-mother's wrath) who so longed for that second scallion. On the other hand, they yearned for the reign of cosmic righteousness (they were not satisfied with human righteousness alone) and its implementation in creation as a whole, again like this orphan boy who prayed that the diminution of the moon be replenished, that the Messiah should come—not on account of his own individual worries, not in order to be redeemed from his bleak existence, from the unbearable burdens weighing down upon him, but on account of his yearnings for the redemption of creation, for the perfection of the cosmos. "I want the moon to become bigger already. It's such a pity on her. True she sinned, but to suffer so much . . . we are already living in the sixth millennium." The orphan forgets that his father will soon take for himself a new wife, a stepmother, and that he will become a stepchild who will have to cry for a piece of bread; he prays for the suffering moon, pining away on account of her sin, and he sees in her torments a cosmic injustice. Is not the image of the Jewish people reflected in such yearnings? Bitter exile and cosmic righteousness, the bleak life of the ghetto and the dream about the replenishment of the new moon, the yearnings for the perfection of creation and ugly poverty—can there be a greater coincidence of opposites?

115. The phrase "a living soul" (*nefesh ḥayyah*) in the verse "And the Lord God formed man of the dust of the ground, and breathed into his nostrils the breath of life; and man became a living soul" (Gen. 2:7) is translated by Onkelos (cf. Rashi, ad loc.) as "speaking spirit"

(*ruaḥ memalela*). Of extreme interest is the statement of Rashi, ad loc. [based upon Gen. Rabbah 14:5]: "'And the Lord God formed [*vay-yitzer*]': [there were] two formations [alluded to by the fact that the word *vay-yitzer* is written here with two *yods*], a formation for this world and a formation for the resurrection of the dead. But in the case [of the formation] of the animal that does not rise for judgment, two *yods* are not written [in the word *va-yitzer*, in Gen. 2:19] in regard to its formation." Cf. Berakhot 61a, Eruvin 18a, Ketubbot 8a, and *Targum Yonatan*, ad loc. See Gen. Rabbah 14:4: "There were two formations; one formation from the lower [realms], one formation from the higher [realms]. . . . He created him with four attributes of lower [creatures]—[i.e., the animals]. He eats and drinks like animals, procreates like animals, excretes like animals, and dies like animals; he stands upright like the ministering angels and speaks, understands, and sees like the ministering angels. . . . R. Tifdai said in R. Aha's name: The higher [creatures] were created in the image and likeness [of God] and do not procreate, while the lower [creatures] procreate, but were not created in [His] image and likeness. Said the Holy One, blessed be He: Behold I will create him [man] in [My] image and likeness; [thus he will partake] of the [character of the] higher [creatures]; while he procreates [as is the nature] of the lower [creatures]. R. Tifdai [also] said in R. Aha's name: The Lord said: If I create him from the higher [elements] [like the angels], he will live [forever] and not die; while if I create him from the lower [elements] [like the animals], he will die and not live [in the world to come]. Therefore, I will create him from the higher [elements] and from the lower [elements]. If he sins, he will die [and be cut off from the world to come]; but if he will not sin, he will live [in the world to come]." The dual nature of man receives particularly clear and sharp expression in these statements.

116. Formation for this world, and formation for the world to come. And is not the world to come dependent upon his deeds? Therefore, if he will sin, he will die; but if not, he will live.

117. Lev. Rabbah 14:1.

118. Maimonides, *Laws of Repentance* 1:1.

119. Kiddushin 49b; Maimonides, *Laws of Marriage* 8:5 (and Maimonides rules there that "she is *doubtfully* betrothed" in accordance with the Talmudic statement "he *may* have had thoughts of repentance in his heart"). Now the ruling under discussion applies even to a case where the man had sinned immediately preceding his statement of betrothal and, therefore, we know for certain that he did not verbally confess. This is the plain meaning of the talmudic text itself, which

states, "he may have had thoughts of repentance in his heart," clearly implying that [in order for the individual to be considered entirely righteous] only thoughts of repentance are required and not verbal confession.

120. See *Minhat hinukh,* Commandment no. 364 [pt. III, p. 10a, in standard editions], which already noted this problem and offered a similar answer. As proof for our contention that the sinner's being divested of his status as a *rasha* is independent of his obtaining atonement, we may cite the fact that while there are four different means of atonement depending upon the gravity of one's sin, as the Talmud (Yoma 86a) states (cf. Maimonides, *Laws of Repentance* 1:4), a sinner requires only repentance and not the other means of atonement [i.e., Day of Atonement, suffering, or death] to regain his status of eligibility as a witness. We must necessarily conclude that the reason why repentance restores the sinner's eligibility as a witness is not because it serves as a means of atonement—for [if the reason why the sinner who repents regains eligibility as a witness is because at the same time he also obtains atonement] then in the case of a person who violated a negative commandment [who requires the Day of Atonement to obtain atonement] we ought also to require the Day of Atonement [in order for him to regain eligibility as a witness], and in the case of a person who violated a commandment carrying with it the penalty of death or excision [who requires suffering in order to obtain atonement] we ought to require suffering as well [for him to regain eligibility], for [in terms of serving as a means of atonement] repentance is on a par with the Day of Atonement and suffering—but, rather, because it divests him of his status as a *rasha* [even in situations where it does not serve as a means of atonement], and for repentance to serve to divest the sinner of his status as a *rasha* it need not be accompanied by verbal confession [which is required only for atonement].

121. Sanhedrin 25b; Maimonides, *Laws of Testimony* 12:4–10.

122. Maimonides would appear to contradict himself with reference to the question as to whether repentance per se always suffices to divest the sinner of his status as a *rasha* or whether in a case where the sinner has incurred the penalty of lashes he must also be flogged by the court in order to be divested of that status. In *Laws of Testimony* 12:4 Maimonides states: "Whoever commits an offense punishable by lashes regains his status of eligibility as soon as he repents or has received lashes"; this would imply that *either* repentance *or* lashes can serve to enable the sinner to regain his status of eligibility. On the other hand, in *Laws of Pleading* 2:10, Maimonides states: "If witnesses testify that

[one suspected with regard to an oath] has received lashes and has repented, he regains his status of eligibility, whether for the purpose of giving testimony or of taking an oath"; this would imply that the sinner, sentenced to lashes, requires *both* lashes *and* repentance in order to regain his status of eligibility. However, this issue does not touch upon the problem under discussion.

123. *Laws of Repentance* 2:2.

124. Ibid., 2:4.

125. See Max Scheler's essay on repentance ["Reue und Wieder-geburt"] in *Vom Ewigen im Menschen* [(Leipzig, 1921), pp. 27–59; "Repentance and Rebirth," in *On the Eternal in Man*, trans. Bernard Noble (London, 1960), pp. 35–65].

126. To be sure, even in other religions a tendency toward the quantification of time can be discerned, but certainly not to the extent prevalent in Judaism.

127. See Scheler, "Repentance and Rebirth"; William Douglas Chamberlain, *The Meaning of Repentance* (Philadelphia, 1943).

128. Maimonides's view regarding the question of the immortality of the nutritive and the vital souls differs, however, from that of Albertus and Thomas, and resembles somewhat the view of Aristotle, this despite the fact that Maimonides disagreed with Aristotle regarding the issue of will. However, this is not the place to elaborate. See Maimonides, *Laws of the Foundations of the Torah* 4:8.

129. This is not the place to analyze the nature of Maimonides's realism regarding the question of universals. However, his view regarding this issue drew upon both the philosophy of Plato and that of Aristotle, and many of the scholastics followed his approach to this problem.

130. Maimonides, *Commentary on the Mishnah*, introduction to *Ḥelek*.

131. *Guide* III, 17.

132. To be sure, even the wicked person (*rasha*) and the fool (*sakhal*) are not to be entirely identified with the man who is merely a random example of the biological species, for the former two are in possession of some good deeds and meritorious acts. See Maimonides, *Laws of Repentance* 8:1: "The good stored up for the righteous is life in the world to come, and it is the life unaccompanied by death and the good unaccompanied by evil. . . . The reward of the righteous is that they will attain this bliss and abide in this [state of] good; the punishment of the wicked is that they will not attain this life but will be cut off and die. He who does not attain this life is the one who is dead, who will never live but is cut off in his wickedness and has perished like the beasts.

And this is the excision referred to in the Torah, as it is said, 'That soul shall be utterly cut off [*hikaret tikaret*], his iniquity shall be upon him' (Num. 15:31), which has been traditionally interpreted (Sanhedrin 62b): 'cut off' [*hikaret*] in this world, 'utterly cut off' [*tikaret*] from the world to come—i.e., that that soul which has separated from its body in this world does not attain life in the world to come but is also cut off from the world to come." And see Nahmanides's discussion of this Maimonidean statement in *Sha'ar ha-gemul* [The gate of reward] [in *Kol Kitvei Ha-Ramban*, ed. C. B. Chavel (Jerusalem, 1963), pp. 291–292].

133. *Guide* III, 17, 18.

134. Maimonides, *Laws of the Foundations of the Torah* 7:1.

135. Maimonides, *Commentary on the Mishnah*, introduction to *Ḥelek*.

136. *Guide* II, 32. "The third opinion [concerning prophecy] is the opinion of our law and the foundation of our doctrine. It is identical with the philosophic opinion except in one thing. For we believe [unlike the philosophers] that it may happen that one who is fit for prophecy and prepared for it should not become a prophet, namely on account of the divine will."

137. *Laws of the Foundations of the Torah* 7:1.

138. *Guide* I, 68. "It is accordingly also clear that the numerical unity of the intellect, the intellectually cognizing subject and the intellectually cognized object, does not hold good with reference to the Creator only, but also with reference to every intellect. Thus in us, too, the intellectually cognizing subject, the intellect, and the intellectually cognized object are one and the same thing whenever we have an intellect *in actu*. We, however, pass intellectually from potentiality to actuality only from time to time ... [while God] is constantly an intellect *in actu* ... and there is absolutely no potentiality in Him." See the discussion of this chapter in Solomon Maimon, *Give'at ha-moreh* [ed. S. H. Bergman and N. Rotenstreich (Jerusalem, 1965), pp. 101–108]; David Neumark, *Toldot ha-filosofiyah be-yisra'el* [vol. 2: *Ḥomer ve-tzurah* (Matter and form) (Philadelphia, 1929), p. 390]; Yehudah [Even-Shmuel] Kaufman, *Commentary on the Guide* [vol. 2 (Jerusalem, 1938) ad loc. (pp. 364–365)].

139. *Guide* II, 32. "As for its being fundamental with us that the prophet must possess preparation and perfection in the moral and rational faculties, it is indubitably the opinion expressed in their [the sages'] dictum: Prophecy only rests upon a wise, strong, and rich man [Shabbat 92a; Nedarim 38a]. We have explained this in our *Commentary on the Mishnah* [in the introduction] and in our great compila-

tion [*Laws of the Foundations of the Torah*], and we have set forth that the *disciples of the prophets* were always engaged in preparation. . . . We find many texts, some of them Scriptural and some of them dicta of the sages, all of which maintain this fundamental principle: that God turns whom He wills, whenever He wills, into a prophet—but only someone perfect and superior to the utmost degree. But with regard to one of the ignorant among the common people, this is not possible according to us: I mean that He should turn one of them into a prophet—except as it is possible that He should turn an ass or a frog into a prophet. It is our fundamental principle that there must be training and perfection, whereupon the possibility arises to which the power of the deity becomes attached." It should be noted that Maimonides admits that there are "obstacle[s] due to temperament" [*Guide* II, 32; cf. I, 34; II, 36] that hinder a person's preparation for prophecy.

140. *Guide* II, 32. "Prophecy is a certain perfection in the nature of man. This perfection is not achieved in any individual from among men except after a training that makes that which exists in the potentiality of the species pass into actuality. . . ."

141. Even the idea of the demiurge (δημιουργός) in Plato's *Timeaus* does not capture the concept of creation in its full sense as the Jewish people understand it. See Paul Deussen, *Die Philosophie der Griechen* [(Leipzig, 1911), pp. 271–272].

142. Nor is Aristotle's recognition of the principle of freedom of the will significant in this context. This freedom does contribute to morphological development, but it does not precipitate an act of creation. Even the ideal of the "Stoic sage" which is given such a prominent—indeed, a too prominent—place in the philosophy of that school does not change the fact that the image of the individual in all its splendor had not yet been conceived. In general the principle of choice is the Achilles' heel both of the doctrine of Aristotle and that of the Stoics. However, this is not the place to elaborate.

143. See above, note 140.

144. This is not the place to discuss Maimonides's doctrine of the nature and value of the affections.

145. Maimonides, *Laws of Repentance* 5:1; cf. *Shemonah Perakim*, chap. 8.

146. A spark of this idea, as it were, made its way into Fichte's philosophy.

147. An echo of the longing for creativity, the ultimate desire of Judaism, makes itself heard in the philosophy of Kant, which is based upon the principle of the spontaneity of the spirit in general, and in

the neo-Kantian school of Hermann Cohen, in the concept of the creative pure thought in particular.

This concept of the obligatory nature of the creative gesture, of self-creation as an ethical norm, an exalted value, which Judaism introduced into the world, reverberates with particular strength in the world views of Kierkegaard, Ibsen, Scheler, and Heidegger. In particular, the latter two set the idea of creation at the very center of their philosophies. Man's ascent from a "psychic I" to a "personal I" (man as a spiritual being) in Scheler's view [as expressed in *Man's Place in Nature*] and his development from "inauthentic existence" to "authentic existence" in the philosophy of Heidegger [as expressed in *Being and Time*] symbolize that norm which aspires to the complete realization of man in the ongoing course of his ontic transformations. However, the fate of Maimonides's idea of creation was similar to the fate of ibn Gabirol's doctrine of the will, as it passed, via Duns Scotus, to Schopenhauer and Nietzsche. Both these ideas, which were pure and holy at their inception, were profaned and corrupted in modern culture. The will was transformed by Schopenhauer into a "blind" will, while for Nietzsche it was embodied in the "superman." Similarly, the longing for creation was perverted into the desire for brutal and murderous domination. Such views have brought chaos and disaster to our world, which is drowning in its blood. See S. H. Bergman's discussion of Ibsen's drama *Peer Gynt* [in "The Philosophy of Martin Heidegger"], *Hogei ha-dor* [(Tel Aviv, 1935), pp. 150–153].